The 7-Day Real Estate Survival Blueprint

The 7-Day Real Estate Survival Blueprint

How to Create $10,000 Out of Nothing in Less Than a Month

Ryan Enk

The 7 Day Real Estate Survival Blueprint
Copyright © 2018 by Ryan Enk

ISBN 978-1-7328739-0-2

Printed in USA by 48HrBooks (www.48HrBooks.com)

DEDICATION

This book is dedicated to the girl who I threw food all over and then asked to marry me. To the one who was riding behind me when I wrecked our rental motorcycle on our honeymoon in Rome and almost killed her. To the one who gave birth to our first child a month after hurricane Katrina hit, who supported me in my unemployment draughts, and let me ride her bike to work when we couldn't afford gas for my truck. She helped me coach a tot's soccer class while she was 9 months pregnant because I had a sprained foot and she supported me through the stress of trying to open an indoor sports arena. She let me try and grow a beard and still kissed me on our anniversary even though she hated it. She cranked out 5 boys with me, and finally let me get rid of all of the baby girl clothes taking up space in our attic.

When we said for rich or for poor, we meant it. When we said for better or for worse, we meant it. We've been through good times and bad. Thank you, Danielle, for putting up with me through food fights, botched motorcycle rides, wealth and poverty, stress and injury, inappropriate comments during child birth, skinny Ryan and fat Ryan, and gross beards. I love you, and I dedicate this book to you.

CONTENTS

PREFACE

Although this plan was inspired by the television series, "Alone", it was written from 15 years' experience of losing everything to gaining the life of my dreams. My very first start in life as an adult was losing everything to Hurricane Katrina.

It was right out of college. What do you do when you pay $20,000 a year for your education? Well, you get a job as a teacher making $24,500 a year of course. This was not exactly a great financial start in the first place for me. But at least it was a "secure" job (or so I thought). It had everything that I was taught that I should want in a job, like a 401k and benefits, etc.

But I remember the feeling of looking at my pay check, and then looking at my bills, and wondering where I was going to cut. I remember living off nothing but cream of wheat and ramen noodles for most meals.

After a year of teaching, I got married, and bought a house. This was my first move to acquiring any sort of wealth. Shortly after getting married, I found out that my wife was pregnant. Eight months after the great news about our first child, I received a call from a friend that I'll never forget. He called with a single question, "Have you seen the news lately?"

Having been distracted and busy with everyday life, I didn't regularly check the news. So, I said, "No I haven't. What's going on?"

He said to me, "We have a category 5 hurricane coming our way. There is a mandatory evacuation."

So I went to Home Depot, bought some boards to protect my house from wind, packed a few of my things and a few of my wife's things and I evacuated on the road to Beaumont, Texas. We were used to hurricane warnings and evacuations in New Orleans. Nothing was really new here. I thought it would probably pass like all the rest and I'd come back home to pick up a few branches.

Boy I was I wrong. The notorious hurricane Katrina hit New Orleans, and my first house that I just purchased several months earlier was underwater and the roof was blown off. All I was left with was my 8-month pregnant wife, a few of our things, a wooden baseball bat I picked up at Walmart to fight off looters just in case, and my Chevy Blazer. All the security that I had been told that I would have went completely out the window.

I remember that my wife, and her entire family had to stay in her brother's college apartment at LSU. And by the way, my wife is the oldest child of 11 kids. So as you can imagine, space was limited in that little apartment. Because there was no room in there for me to sleep, I slept in my Chevy Blazer. And because we were rationing gasoline, I had to sleep next to the gas cans I had filled up earlier that day. I remember trying to sleep with half my head out of the window and the rest of my body inside, so I didn't have to smell the fumes.

The school where I had been teaching was now 6 feet underwater, meaning I was now unemployed. I couldn't believe my new reality, that I was an unemployed, homeless husband to an 8-month pregnant wife. I felt like I was failing at the whole "providing for your family" part of fatherhood before it even started.

Then, since I didn't have a job, I started going on job interviews to see if I could find employment. That college degree I invested in was supposed to give me security in having some sort of job when I needed one. Well now, I really REALLY needed one.

If there is anything that I got really good at, it was getting told "no" for jobs that I interviewed for. So I thought to myself, "Well I've got no other choice. If nobody else is going to hire me, then I have to hire myself." So I started my own business.

By this point in my life, I've determined I was really was good at getting told "no" for jobs that I interviewed for AND sucking at trying to start my own business. I made so many mistakes I lost count. I even hired a drug addict, who went on to steal $4,000 from me and skipped town for Australia. This wasn't exactly what I would call a stellar return on my investment!

I remember literally reaching into the couch cushion if my family wanted to go out to eat, to see if I could find enough loose change to afford going out to a fast food restaurant.

I remember that my wife was invited to go on an all girl's weekend in Florida. While all the other wives and ladies were going with cash, check, or credit, I handed my wife a Kentwood bottle that was 10% full of change and told her that was the budget we had for the weekend. I remember how small I felt in doing that, and how inadequate I felt as a husband, father, and provider.

I finally got a corporate job selling copiers. Although I learned a lot about business and negotiations, it was a miserable job. I don't know if you've ever seen that movie from the 90s called "Office Space", but in the movie, they took the copier out to the field and beat it with a bat. That's how most people felt about me as I would walk through their door uninvited to sell them a copier. I felt like I had all kinds of gifts and talents, but they were going to waste by doing something every day that I didn't enjoy. Not only did I not enjoy it, but it also gave me a tremendous amount of stress and anxiety that made life difficult.

But what was worse, it seemed like the harder I worked the poorer we were. We were what you call just over broke (J.O.B. for short). But most times it was just flat out broke. I turned to selling some of our stuff in garage sales to try to make ends meet. I was working 12 to 14-hour days with not really a break anywhere. And even when I came home, I wasn't totally present with my wife and kids, which to me, was the worst part of all of it.

I finally hit my breaking point when I sold a Catholic Monastery a copier and the monk called me to chew me out because something didn't work on it. I thought to myself, "This is IT! I'm in a real bad place if I'm sitting here getting chewed out by monks."

I had nothing. But something had to give. And I asked myself a question that would change my life forever. And that question was this, "What would you do if money didn't matter"? And I thought, well if money didn't matter, I would open up an indoor sports arena for soccer and flag football, or I'd play music or something.

I had never discussed this with my wife before, so I called her and had a conversation with her about it. I said, "Hey babe, as you know I'm wrestling with daily anxiety in this job and it's STILL not paying the bills. Let's say money didn't matter. Let's pretend we had a million dollars. What could you see me doing if money wasn't such an issue?"

And without hesitation she said, "I don't know. Maybe opening up an indoor sports arena or playing music or something like that."

We had NEVER spoken of a dream like this before, so I took this as a sign from God. It was at this moment that I decided that I was going to seek another way, and I went on a quest to start replacing my working income, so I could pursue the indoor arena dream.

The problem was that I had no idea where to start. I knew that "working harder" couldn't be the solution. I was already a hard worker. And if working hard was all it took to be rich, then coal miners would be millionaires. I needed to work smarter. So, I started picking up books on how to make money.

Thankfully, I stumbled across Robert Kiyosaki's book called "Rich Dad Poor Dad" and it shifted my mindset and my approach. Instead of exchanging my time for money. I was going to invest in assets that would provide for me "passive income".

I chose real estate as a way to do this. First of all, because I was always hearing about these multi-millionaires who made their money with real estate. But second, because I was learning that you could get started with no money, no bank loans, or experience if you did it the right way. For a broke dude like me, that was right up my ally.

So if I could just find a way to acquire a property, I had so many opportunities for a payday:

1) I could buy it below the market value and "flip" it for profit.
2) I could "cash flow" on the difference between the rental payments and my payments on the house.
3) I could grow in wealth by getting a renter to pay down my debt on the amortization of a loan.
4) The market could appreciate, and I would gain more net worth for when I decided to sell.
5) If I DID get to the point where I was making lots of money, I could use "paper depreciation" to offset my taxable income.

There are more advanced opportunities to make other "pay days" with real estate, but for me, this was a good starting point I decided that I needed to pursue in order to get out of the rat race.

So, the first thing I did that launched me into financial freedom, was I started educating myself on real estate investing strategies. I read book after book on how to buy real estate. I took classes and online courses. Everything that I learned, I did.

Sometimes I would try and fail. But ultimately, those failures led to other much greater successes. But I started learning by moving forward and taking action. I didn't start with any money to my name. But I bought house after house after house. I wholesaled. I flipped. I bought residential property. I did apartments. I bought commercial property. I bought short term vacation rentals. Finally, my dream came true. And not only did I buy a 2-million-dollar indoor sports arena, but also a year later, I bought another one.

But that didn't stop my real estate activity. I did creative and owner financing. I also did what I call "Rolling Real Estate", which is renting out RVs on the short-term rental market. I bought a coworking space. Started a real estate investment club. You name a strategy in real estate investing and I have probably done it.

Once I figured out how to piece all of the real estate strategies into one powerful strategy that made the most money in the shortest amount of time with the lowest risk and the most opportunity for passive income, the result was that in less than 12 months, I grew my net worth to over a million dollars. I was able to create enough "passive income" to quit my job. I made enough passive income for my wife to no longer have to work her job as a nurse, and within my own business, I was able to fire myself, which was an even better feeling than firing my boss. I was able to spend more time with my family and take RV trips across the country. I was able to buy a yacht at the foreclosure sale and take a family trip down to Destin and back. And lastly, I was able to buy my dream home on the river, where I live today with my wife, 5 kids (all boys...I don't know how to make girls), and a stupid dog that you can steal from me in the middle of the night if you want her.

But most importantly, real estate investing has allowed me to look at each of my days from 500 feet up instead of 5 inches in front of my face in the rat race. It's allowed me to figure out how I was going to use my gifts and talents to serve others. I could play the music for my kid's Church on Monday morning weekdays. I could raise money for various charities that I'm involved in. And I can mentor other people to success.

SO here is the thing...I'm not anybody that is particularly special. You might think that in order for me to have these accomplishments, I might have a level of talent or intelligence beyond yours. Well...let me assure you, I don't. I wasn't particularly great in school. Nobody would ever accuse me of being "scholarship material". I didn't make the best decisions. Actually, I almost got arrested for mooning a cop. But if someone like me, who was stupid enough to wave his butt cheeks out of the window at a sheriff can achieve this, then so can you.

I have created for you the ultimate blueprint with this book. You don't have to make the mistakes I made. I've condensed 15 years' worth of lived experience going from broke to being financially free using real estate into a 7-day battle plan. All you have to do, is follow the plan.

INTRODUCTION: Starting from Ground Zero

Here's the scenario…

You suddenly lose everything but a few dollars. You have a laptop and a Wi-Fi connection, or cell phone, and a clean pair of casual clothes. Bills are piling up. Creditors are pounding at your door. You have no money. You have no credit to borrow on. You have a family that is depending on you to provide. And you have 30 days to make 10k to survive. How do you do it?

This real estate 7-day survival blueprint was inspired by the TV Series, "Alone". The premise of this show is that they have 10 contestants that are all dropped off in the middle of nowhere in the woods on Vancouver Island. Contestants are given no money, no stores, nothing. Just a backpack full of survival gear. The winner will be the one who can survive alone the longest against all the external elements of nature such as the wild bears, wolves, cougars, and grueling winter weather and wind. But that's the easy part. The real champion will be the one that conquers all of the internal elements as well: love vs fear, hope vs despair, and giving up vs. perseverance. And that winner, makes $500,000.

Just like "Alone", real estate is a game of mindset, strategy, and skills.

The survivalist and the real estate investor both have to be **mentally strong**. They have to be resourceful with what they have available to them on their little section of earth. They have to be grateful for every little success, and not be discouraged but instead strengthened by failures.

Strategy plays a major role for the real estate investor and the survivalist. What do you pursue first, if you start with nothing? Shelter? Food? Fresh water? What you prioritize has a huge impact on your survival. The real estate investor needs to figure out what's going to make the most money right NOW. You have only have 30 days to make 10k. But you can't just do one real estate deal and quit. You have to set yourself up for the long haul as well. The survivalist needs to have the land produce food for him over and over again. He can't just catch one fish with a pole and call it quits. He needs to find an area of his cove that he can harvest food or put out a gill net and bring in fish on a consistent basis. If he can't, he's out. You need to be efficient at how you choose your strategy for real estate both short term and long term. You can't just flip one house. You'll be in the same situation you were in last month. You need a long-term plan that will produce cash for you on a consistent basis. And even though you need 10K NOW, you also need to start NOW developing passive income. In this way, you can switch from "surviving" to actually "living".

And last, but not least, the survivalist and the investor need to have or quickly adapt the right skills. Anybody can make a tent. You just need to know how. Anybody can make a mouse trap. You just need to know how. Anybody can make a fire. You just need to know how. It's the same with real estate. Anybody can find money, find deals, and market property. You just need to know how.

Real estate is not a talent. A talent is something you are born with. There is nothing you can do to control that. A skill, however, is different from a talent. ANYBODY can learn a skill with education and practice.

It's important to note here, that there is all kind of ways to approach real estate. You can definitely speed things up by paying for services such as MLS, mailing out marketing pieces, marketing for cash buyers and private money lenders, or marketing for motivated sellers. But the premise of this 7-day battle plan is that you are starting from NOTHING. I firmly believe, that even if you HAVE MONEY, if you just go through this exercise and pretend like you don't, you will be tremendously successful speeding things up with money. It's like training to run fast by running up hill. Your muscles develop because of the resistance that they undergo. Once you start running on a level playing field, without resistance, you will run faster than you would if you trained on the flat surface.

How to Get the Best Use Out of This Daily Blueprint:

I've written this for you as an exercise. It's designed to be accomplished in 7 days, but everyone's circumstances are different. You may get through it sooner, or it may take you a bit longer. The timing is ultimately up to you. Just remember to be flexible and work your schedule according to your current situation. But no matter what, don't get discouraged by timeframes. This isn't designed to be a rigid schedule (we're not in school anymore). Just stick with it, no matter how long it takes you to accomplish it. I promise you, it will be worth it.

But you need to be disciplined to fit this into your current schedule. We can all find an extra 30 minutes per day to dedicate to changing our lives forever. You're about to learn skills that will provide for you for the rest of your life. I suggest you make the rest of your life a priority and block out 30 minutes per day. You might not accomplish this in 7 days. You might not accomplish this in less than 30 days. But you will still make the progress you need to make in order to be more financially free in the future.

I also recommend reading through the entire plan once to have a good understanding of how the entire plan plays out, just like a good builder would look at an entire blueprint of a house before he starts pouring the slab. Once you're finished reviewing the whole thing, you can go back and put the action items on your own personal calendar with your own personal time frames and execute.

DAY 1
Casting Your Nets

5am- Wake Up- Why so early?   Because the most successful people in the world wake up early.   It's the only time in the day where you can avoid all distractions and get focused.   Your success today will depend on how you set your mindset in the morning.   This exact time (5am) will depend on your CURRENT routine and how easy it is for you to adjust. If you can't start out on day one waking up at 5am, try at least waking up an hour earlier than when you usually wake up and adjust your schedule from there.   Set the alarm and wake up on the dot. Don't hit snooze. Hitting snooze is like losing the first battle of the day.

5:00-5:05am- Make Coffee- You may not need this. But I definitely do. Also, I used to make my coffee with a crap load of cream and sugar. Now I just drink it straight black. I do this because I utilize "fasting" as a method to increase my focus in the morning. Basically, I don't eat from

8pm at night to 2pm the next day. When you have sugar in the morning, your insulin spikes and your body focuses more on digestion than it does on repairing and replenishing all the other cells in your body. So, I start with just black coffee. It was gross at first. But I got used to it. By doing so, and then not eating until 2pm, my body can focus on repairing and replenishing all the other cells in my body instead of digesting. Because of this, my brain is like the super version of itself in the morning. Try it and see the difference in your mental clarity.

5:05am-5:35am- Pray/Meditate/Reflect- This is a critical part of your focus. If you are not a praying person, you can just meditate on a few elements. But praying for me is like plugging into my energy source at the beginning of the day. I do this with my wife, and I HIGHLY recommend doing this with your spouse to increase your unity through this process. There are 4 powerful elements in your daily prayer and meditation that will positively change the course of your day, and by default, also change your life, if done habitually. Here are the 4 elements:

Gratitude- First and foremost, express and reflect on what you are grateful for. When you are thankful for what you have, you get more. When you're ungrateful you get less. If you have kids, you understand this concept. When your kids are grateful for what they have, it makes you want to be more generous to them. When they aren't you start wanting to take away the iPad, and all the other things they take for granted. Life is the same way. Life tends to reward gratitude.

In the show "Alone", when someone was grateful for catching a fish after 3 days of not eating, they carried that energy of gratitude with them for everything else they subsequently did. All of a sudden, that gratitude affected the way they carved a spear, lit their fires, trapped food, etc. Gratitude, gives you the energy you need to accomplish your goals. So, I meditate deeply on EVERYTHING I am grateful for, from the coffee that wakes me up, to the breath in my lungs, to what's in my bank account (even if it's barely anything).

Reflection- I read an excerpt from the Bible and reflect on it somedays. Other days, I will watch an inspirational video. I have daily inspirational videos coming into my Facebook feed from Goalcast and other various motivational pages a subscribe to. My goal here is to carry with me some sort of inspirational message that will fuel me mentally throughout the day and cause me to keep going where I might otherwise want to stop. I think of this reflection like taking a bite of an amazingly favorable piece of steak. You don't want to just chomp down on it twice and swallow. You want to chew that steak for a while and let the flavors marinade in your mouth, so you can enjoy every last morsel of it. The reflection in the morning of the wisdom and inspiration you tap into should be the same way. Read one sentence, and let it sink in before moving to the next. Watch the video, let it sink in, reflect, then watch it again. Whatever you can do to get full impact of that steak.

Intentions- I visualize what I want, and I ask God for it. I spend a great deal of time imagining what it's like to find a deal, negotiate with a seller, and talk to a cash investor. Then I imagine what it's like to hold the $10,000 check in my hand. This isn't hokey pokey stuff. This is simple brain programming. Your brain is like what they call a "Servo Mechanism" in the military. It's basically like a heat seeking missile. You program the coordinates of where you want to go, and the missile (your brain) will naturally navigate around any obstacles until it hits its goals. You will even do this without realizing you are doing it if you program your brain the right way first thing in the morning.

Plan- There is a lot of ways to plan, digital and hard copy. I personally do better with paper. So I always sit down with two notebooks. One is for collecting all my thoughts and tasks and writing down all my goals. The other is a planner for organizing them into a daily structure. I use a "Freedom Planner". The best was to make your goal-setting effective is to use a process called "reverse engineering". Start with the goal in mind and work backward. Your goal today is do what you need to do TODAY, in order to have $10,000 in your bank account in less than a month from now.

5:35am-6:05am- Exercise and stretch. Working out increases mental clarity, gets the endorphins running, and energizes you to accomplish today's tasks.

6:05am-7:05am- Work on the strategy that is best for today.

In the show "Alone", the contestants had to figure out what they were going to focus on that day. Were they going to find fresh water? Were they going to find shelter? Were they going to find food? Were they going to find out where the best place to make a fire would be? The best strategists in the show were able to do all of it in the same day at the same time.

Thankfully, in real estate there are two simple strategies one can take: The "Quick Nickle" or the "Slow Dime". Quick Nickel is taking less-time to get a smaller profit, for example flipping a house or wholesaling a contract. "Slow Dime" is a more passive income strategy, where you use time to accumulate a greater amount of wealth- purchasing a rental property for instance.

What we are going to have to do is find a combination of both of these strategies in order to make $10,000 in less than a month. But like we discussed, you don't just want to be one and done. So a good goal for long-term passive income building would be to make at least $200 or more that will come into your bank account every single month without you doing anything. You want the passive income to set yourself up for financial freedom in the long-term, while satisfying your short-term needs.

We also need to take in consideration that since we only have 30 days, we can't use the banks. Even if you have good credit, it's going to take too long to get approved for a loan and cut through their red tape.

Since our time is limited and we have set a goal for $10,000- the options are limited and are often not part of what one would consider traditional real estate investing. We have to either use a technique called "wholesaling" or another method that requires mathematical creativity called a "sandwich lease option". We COULD find a private money lender this month through this process, but we're not going to depend on that. The good news is, in trying to execute the wholesale deal and creative finance deal, we could stumble across an incredible source of cash from a private money lender that we will be able to use in subsequent months.

So what is wholesaling? Wholesaling is where you go out and look for discounted properties from motivated sellers. Say you find, for example, a property from someone who is going through a divorce, so they are motivated to sell quick. And that property is worth $150,000, but they are willing to sell it for $100,000. What you would do is get that property under contract for $100,000 and then find a bunch of cash buyers. Then you will send a message to your list of cash buyers that says something to the effect of, "I've got a house worth $150,000 that I can sell to you for $110,000 in cash. Are you interested?" Once you have an interested Cash Buyer who wants to buy the house for $110,000 or more, you do either a "double closing" or a "contract assignment" and make $10,000 on a house you got signed under contract. You didn't buy the house. You just found the deal, got it under contract, and sold it to another cash buyer for a profit. Pretty cool, right?

Ok, let's talk about the sandwich lease option. This is what is known as "owner financing". Similar to wholesaling, you start this strategy by looking for discounted properties from motivated sellers as well. However, instead of getting a bank to give you a loan to buy the property, the owner finances the property to you themselves using a lease option. Owner financing can work EVEN IF the owner has a mortgage on the property. Next, instead of you selling the property to someone who has bank financing, you lease option it to them as well. So you both buy a property with a lease option, and you sell it with a lease option. The way this pans out will become clearer to you as we go over specific examples in later chapters.

In the show "ALONE", the contestants could pick their weapons, but they had to pick carefully because they only had room for a few things in their survival pack. Do you take the fishing pole, the cast net, the floating gill net, a bow and arrow, or a hatchet?

The same decision must be made with real estate. You can use many different kinds of legal contracts to owner finance a deal. These options include a credit sale, a deed in lieu, a bond for deed, a land contract, or a lease option. Because you only have 30 days to execute both the purchase and the sale, the best weapon of choice is the lease option. You can buy today with it, and sell tomorrow with it, without having to go through closing costs, title search, etc. If you haven't gotten a lease option contract yet or the supplemental training on how to use it, the resource page in the back of this book will show you how to get it.

This strategy is a "little" more involved than the wholesaling, but if you can nail this strategy, you will not only make the $10k you need, but you'll also create for yourself long-term passive income. So, for example, you find a motivated seller who is going through bankruptcy. They have a house worth $250,000 that they are willing to sell to you for $187,000. Their mortgage, taxes, and insurance are $1500 a month. But rents in the area are $2000 a month. They also have $5000 in back payments that they need to catch up on with the bank. What you are going to do is offer them as a purchase price $187,000, PLUS pay $5000 in their back payments, and take over $1500 a month in payments. This is going to be a winning situation for them. Because by you paying off their back payments and consistently paying their monthly note, you will improve their credit.

You might be thinking right now, "Wait a minute Ryan...You told me you could do this with no money but now you're telling me I need $5000 to catch them up?" Here's what you do. You get the property under contract under those terms and give yourself 15 days for an inspection period. During that time, you will find a lease to own buyer for that property. Ideally, what we are going to do is have a few buyers already lined up. So once you get this house under contract, you will just bring it to a buyer that has at least $5000 for a down payment. Then you turn around and use that $5000 to execute the contract between you and the motivated seller going through bankruptcy. In this way, you just acquired a property with no money out of your own pocket.

You might be thinking, "Who buys houses on lease options?" Think about this: What is common when you purchase a house? With a conventional loan, you have to pay 20% of the value of the home as a down payment. So for a $250,000 home that down payment would be $50,000.

What you will do is market to people that want to buy a $250,000 home, but they just don't have $50,000. Maybe they don't have the 20% the bank wants. Maybe they don't have the W2 income that the banks like to see. But maybe they work for themselves and still make good money. Or maybe they have a little bit of credit repair that makes them too big of a risk in the eyes of the bank. BUT, maybe they have 10%. That's $25,000. Maybe they have 7.5%. That's $18,750. Maybe they have 5%. That's $12,500. And they are willing to put that money down on a $250,000 house so that they can stop throwing their money away on rent and become a home owner again. With the banks tightening up on lending, there is a surprisingly large number of people that fit into this category.

Do you see where I'm going with this? If you've only got 30 days, all you need to do is find the motivated seller that is willing to owner finance, and pair that up with a buyer that needs owner financing. If you can do that, you can easily make $10,000 this month. PLUS, this situation has the added benefit of giving you monthly passive income in the form of the rent payment minus the monthly payment. For example, this motivated seller might make a deal with you where you pay them $1500 a month. However, houses in the area rent out for $2000 a month. On this deal, you would be making $500 a month of passive income ($2000-$1500).

So those are the two strategies we are going to use to provide us with $10k as soon as possible, and hopefully, some long-term passive income as well. The first strategy is wholesaling. And the second strategy is the sandwich lease option.

And that brings us to today. What do we prioritize? Well, there is ONE common theme in BOTH of these strategies. And that is.... motivated sellers and potential cash buyers or owner financed buyers. Looks like we're gonna go fishing today for 3 different kinds of fish: 1) Motivated Sellers, 2) Cash Buyers, 3) Owner Financed Buyers.

In the show, the contestants used a variety of ways to catch fish. There was active fishing with a pole. And there was setting nets, traps, and lines in the water and coming back to it later to see if they brought anything in.

What are we going to do? Active searching, or putting lines in the water? We've only got 30 days! We're doing both! So let's spend the next hour prepping how we are going to catch these fish.

7:05am-7:35am- Find Out Where All of the Fish Are Hanging Out

Selecting where you are going to set up camp is extremely important. You want to look for areas near the water where there is tide, vegetation and activity so that you have the best chance of finding something to eat. You don't want to set up in areas of desolation. If you were to walk to an area of earth with lots of birds flying around or in the water, fish jumping, plants growing, bear tracks and dead fish carcasses, then you are probably in a very fruitful zip code of the wilderness. Where animals are eating other animals is actually where you want to be.

In real estate, we want to see where all of the Cash Buyers are investing. You don't have to recreate the wheel and do a detailed analysis of rents and ROI profits in the area. You just have to follow where all the other cash buyers are investing. They already did the work for you. Finding the zip codes where the Cash Buyers are buying will tell you a) Where you are going to the find the most deals that make the most financial sense, and b) When you get a deal under contract in this area, you will have a pool of Cash Buyers that you can market to who you already know are interested in investing in the area.

So how do you know which zip codes have the most Cash Buyers? I'm going to teach your right now this awesome secret trick on how to do it for free.

Step 1) Go to Listsource.com and create an account. It's free.

Step 2) Click "Build a List".

Step 3) Select "County".

Step 4) Select your state.

Step 5) Ad the county where you want to find cash buyers.

Step 6) Go to the upper tab "properties".

Step 7) Under "select criteria" select "Equity %".

Step 8) Select 91%-100% and hit "add". This will show you who has 91 to 100% equity in their property, meaning that they are a cash buyer.

Step 9) Next in the drop-down menu, select "Property Types".

Step 10) Select Single Family Residential and hit "Add". You can also add duplex and 4 plex if you want.

Step 11) Drop down to the "Last Market Sales Date" and select the last 6 months and hit add. This will give you a list of everyone who has bought houses in cash as early as the last 6 months.

Step 12) Click the "options" tab.

Step 13) Click Absentee Owned- This means they bought the property in cash, but they are not living in the property. This indicates that they are an investor.

Step 14) Hit "No preference" under trustee-owned properties & corporate owned properties.

Step 15) Click "mailing address complete". On the left-hand side, it will tell you how many properties have been bought in cash from investors in the last 6 months in your area. It will look something like this:

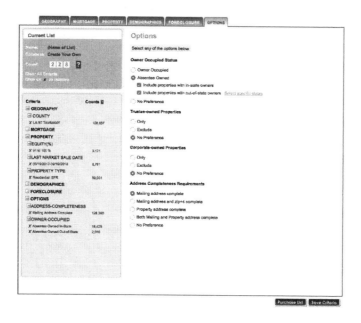

As you can see, in my areas search, there were 228 properties that had been bought in cash from investors in the last 6 months.

Now, what we want to do is find out the most popular zip codes that the properties were purchased in. That will tell us where we need to focus our real estate efforts. So…

Step 16) Click "Purchase list". You're not going to actually purchase it unless you have money to do so. If you DO have money for this, then go ahead and purchase it because this will be your cash buyers list that you can call on to see if they want to be added to your database. If not, no worries. We're going to use other free methods.

Step 17) It will give you the option to "Purchase Partial List". Click that.

Step 18) Select "Custom Selection".

Step 19) Select "zip codes".

Step 20) It will show you which zip codes have the most active cash buyers. THIS will be where you want to focus your efforts.

Step 21) Click "export" then email it to yourself.

Step 22) Go to your email and download the list.

Step 23) On the excel sheet click "sort" and it should show you largest to smallest

BOOM! You now know where to set up camp! Look at that excel sheet and see which zip codes have the most active cash buyers in them. These zip codes are your real estate honey-hole and where you will be focusing your efforts.

8:05am-9:05am- We're going to get started by fishing for some Motivated Sellers. Look how much we've accomplished today, and it's only 8:05am! Paying for leads would be a great way to find motivated sellers. But we don't have time or money for that right now. We need to focus our attention on the lowest hanging fruit that comes from free sources.

We're going to get out an excel spreadsheet, or a piece of paper if you don't have excel, and we're going to make a list of ALL potential motivated sellers. As a side note, I think it's worth mentioning that many new real estate investors use an app called "Podio". I don't personally use it cause I'm a little old school when it comes to managing my leads. Excel and paper have always just been the most effective for me. But if you prefer to keep track of things digitally, Podio is the most popular free CRM source for real estate investors. For the sake of this exercise, just humor me and pretend that excel is all you have.

Our goal for this hour is to create the biggest possible list of motivated sellers. If I have one pole in the water, I'm going to be limited to how many fish I can bring in. So I want as many lines in the water as possible. Because this is strictly a numbers game. The larger the number of lines, the larger the chance of pulling in a fish. So our goal right now is to have the longest list possible of potential motivated sellers.

Our spreadsheet will simply have these categories in the picture below, so we can keep track of where we are with each property.

The only thing that we are going to focus on right now is the address, name of seller (may not be able to get it right away), Number and Email of Seller (either one will work, but preferably both), what the house is listed for, and what we think it's worth. All the other things we will fill out once we actually contact the sellers.

The first and easiest thing we're going to do is hop on Craigslist.org. If there are any fish to be caught in this pond, we're going to catch them! Click on your closest city and then under the category of housing, click "real estate for sale". I personally prefer the "gallery view", but it may be easier for you to do the map view to match up with the most popular zip codes you just found.

Next, we're going to start searching certain key words that could possibly tip us off to there being a motivated seller. We're going to search for the following keywords:

- Motivated
- Motivated seller
- Investor
- Investor special
- Owner financing
- Owner financed
- Owner financing available
- Bring all offers
- Make an offer
- Offer
- Must sell

- Priced to Sell
- Reduced
- Moving
- New job
- Relocating
- Sell fast
- Fast
- Renovation opportunity
- Opportunity

Each house that comes up under these terms, we will populate in our spreadsheet or notebook. Do this for every area you are comfortable doing business in. It may be just your city, or you can spread it to another city you wouldn't mind driving to. Personally, I try to keep everything within an hour driving distance from me.

The next thing we are going to do on Craigslist is look for people who are sick of being landlords. They already have their house listed for rent, but they may be interested in selling. We won't know until we contact them. This is one of the most valuable but yet overlooked sources of motivated sellers. I guarantee you, any competition you might have is not using this technique. The thing is, because the landlord is already ready to rent out the place, he may be open to an "owner financed" offer to buy. The only difference between that and the landlord's current situation, is that with what you would offer, he wouldn't have any of the headaches of the renters, maintenance and upkeep. You will take that on yourself. But really, you can owner finance the property and make the upkeep the responsibility of the tenant buyer. OR, if there is enough wiggle room in the deal, you can get a property manager.

A property manager is the secret to making a property "Passive". For me, it's not even worth getting a property if I can't afford to have a property manager maintain it and deal with renters. When you start talking to these landlords, you want to find out if they are managing the property themselves or if they have a property manager. If they are managing the property themselves, you may have a real hot lead, because they are probably sick of dealing with typical landlord issues. They should be letting someone else handle them. But most times, they refuse to let someone else control the property.

"Why pay someone else to do something when I can do it myself and save money?" You'll hear this line from landlords that want to get out of the game. Why pay someone else? Because now you have your time and your life back. Now you have time to go find more deals and make even more money. That's why. But don't tell them that. Ha! Just let them owner finance it to you and be done with all the "headaches".

Go back to the home page of Craigslist, and this time click "Apartments/Housing", and begin to populate your list with everyone who is advertising their house for rent. When you are populating your list, make sure that you put some sort of notation on it that this is a current landlord, so that you know how to talk to them. Scan through ALL rentals available. What you are looking for is anything that is a single-family home or multifamily home. But you want to avoid the huge commercial apartment complexes. You're going to waste your time calling a property manager for a big complex.

9:05am-9:35am- Set your lines for Motivated Sellers.

The next thing that we are going to do, is go to iftt.com. Those letters stand for "If This Than That". It is a website that basically scrapes Craigslist for keywords. A "scraper" is basically an automated computer program that scours the internet for certain words. So anytime somebody posts a new house on Craigslist in your area with those keywords that you previously searched for, you can set it, so they will automatically send you an email. So, you get the leads with these keywords as soon as somebody posts them to Craigslist, and you can be the first person to contact them. So go to iftt.com and get set up to receive automatic email updates when someone lists a house on Craigslist with any of the above keywords.

9:35am-9:50am Start to Create Your Cash Buyers List

There are lists that you can pay for that will show you how to find people in your area that are buying houses in cash. But you don't have money for that right now, so you will have to employ some guerilla tactics. Here's what's awesome about that though. These guerrilla tactics I'm about to show you will pay you dividends in the long run, and you will have way more success with them if you do them right because you will develop some key relationships with people that will help grow your real estate investing business in the future.

Again, you are just going to create a basic list that you want to start populating using either an excel spreadsheet or a notebook. Create something like this below:

9:50am-10:00am- Put a line in the water on Craigslist to attract some Cash Buyers

What you want to do is create a basic ad. You're going to create it in the for sale>wanted>by owner category. It will say something like this:

Headline: Looking for a cash investor for real estate deals

Content: I am a real estate investor, but sometimes I get more deals than I have cash to execute myself. If you're interested in receiving deals as they come in, please contact me.

10:00am-11:00am- Call everyone who advertised themselves on craigslist as an investor and ask them if they want to be added to your buyers list if you have a discount property. The conversation should look something like this:

You: Hey (name), how are you? My name is _____ < I'm a local real estate investor and I saw your ad on Craigslist that you were an investor as well. Sometimes I come across discount properties that I can't always fund with my own cash, so I am looking to grow a network of other investors that I can send deals to when I get them if I can't fund them. Are you okay with me sending you deals I come across?

Them: Yes...

You: Great, where would you like me to send them? What email? What types of properties do you invest in? Do you normally rehab, or do you just buy and hold? What price range are you looking for?...........Cool. Awesome to meet you over the phone. I hope we get to do business on a deal in the future.

So go onto Craigslist and just search for "investor", "investor looking", "investor seeking", or "cash investor" and call on the people who have put ads out. Even if they say they are a business, or restaurant, or a something else investor. EVERYONE is normally interested in real estate.

There is one thing you need to be aware of though. There will probably be other wholesalers in your area who may put up ads like "Cash Investor Looking for Distressed Properties" or "We Buy Houses Fast with Cash". They don't have cash themselves. They are just trying to attract motivated sellers to answer the ad so that they can get the house under contract and sell to another cash buyer, same as you. This is nothing to be worried about. You just have to understand that some people that you call may be wholesalers themselves.

If you're a long-term thinker, it would be good for you to develop a relationship with any wholesalers you come across and ask them to ad you to their buyers list. I know, you don't have cash right now. But when you get cash, you are going to transition your strategy. Instead of wholesaling properties to other cash investors, you will buy the properties and hold onto them for passive income cashflow. When you get to this phase, instead of you going out and finding all the discount properties yourself, you can have a wholesaler bring them to you.

11am-12pm- Be resourceful with what you already have in your network to find Cash Buyers.

Start with your "inner circle". This is people that already know who you are. Then move to people whom you have mutual friendships with. What you're looking for is anybody that may have some cash they want to invest. It could be a doctor or a dentist friend. It could be Aunt May. It could be your buddy from college that just won the lottery. You're looking for ANYONE who may have cash, knows that they need to diversify their portfolio outside of the volatile stock market, but doesn't have time to go find real estate deals.

So here's what you're going to do. Open up your Facebook and LinkedIn Accounts and start creating a list of everyone who MAY have some cash to invest $25k or more. Once you are done creating that list, call or message EVERY SINGLE ONE with a message similar to this:

You: Hey Buddy/Aunt May/Dave, how are you doing? How's the family (blah blah blah).......great! Hey listen, I'm starting to do some real estate investing. I don't know what your current cash situation is, but I'm starting to find some really awesome real estate investing opportunities with some pretty great returns. When I come across these, are you interested in me showing them to you to see what the investment opportunity might look like?

Them: Of course!

You: Great! If I come across something, maybe we can grab some lunch or coffee or beer sometime and we can discuss the details.

If they say, "not right now", a good response is, "No problem. Do you know of anyone else that might be interested in investing in real estate? Do you mind if I give them a call and mention that I know you?"

To be clear, you may be able to find two types of cash buyers here. They could be someone that you can wholesale a contract to, OR they could be your private money lender that will help you buy a property and hold onto it for cash flow. If they have the money, but don't want to flip the house themselves, then they can just lend it to you at a fixed interest rate.

The details here aren't important right now. You just need to know when you talk to them if they are interested in taking on the property themselves to flip or hold and rent out, or if they are interested in just being a silent investor with you managing the property's profits. This book doesn't cover that stage of the game where you have in hand a private money lender. But it helps you get there. Once you're there, you have hit the fast track to financial freedom. I only mention it in this book because while our goal right

NOW is survival, we need to focus NOW on doing the things that set us up for financial freedom in less than a year from now.

12pm-1pm- Start your networking efforts for Cash Buyers.

Go onto BiggerPockets.com and create a profile. Search for cash investors in your area and introduce yourself and see if you can add them to your list.

Google "Real Estate Investment Club" in your locality and put on your calendar when the next meeting is and attend. Oh look! It's this WEDNESDAY coming up. With most of these clubs, everyone is able to introduce themselves at the beginning of the meeting and say what their real estate goals are. The best networking advice here is to keep it short and sweet. You want your introduction to look something like this:

"Hi, my name is Ryan and I'm a local investor. I currently have some properties that I am negotiating at a pretty deep discount. I don't always use my own money to buy them, and I'm not really interested in rehabbing. So if anyone here is a cash investor that is interested in rehabbing or being a private money lender with a first lien position on a discount property, I'd love to connect with you."

1pm-3pm- Take a Field Trip Down to the Courthouse

Every once in a while, when you're fishing, you can find your honey hole. The honey hole is the place that is going to give you all kinds of fish at almost every cast. The courthouse is your honey hole. It is an absolute gold mine of both Cash Buyers and Motivated Sellers if you know where to look.

The next most important thing you are going to do today is make a visit down to the courthouse. If you don't know where it is, just simply do a google search for "civil sheriff foreclosure sale (your county)".

Have you ever heard the phrase "kill two birds with one stone"? Well, you are going to kill like 7 birds with one stone during this visit to the courthouse:

First item on the agenda: You are going to learn when the civil sheriff foreclosure sales take place so that you can put in your calendar to visit the live auctions. You may or may not have cash by this time to participate in the sales. That's ok.

Because guess who shows up to these things? That's right...Cash Buyers. You need to have all cash to participate in civil sheriff foreclosure sales. The bait is set by the court, and all you need to do is show up and cherry pick the Cash

Buyers. You will find cash buyers that do rehabs, cash buyers who buy and hold, and cash buyers who may also be willing to be your private money lender in the future. You want to meet ALL OF THEM after the bidding is over. Don't be intimidated by the fact that they have so much money. In my experience, they are like the nicest people on the planet, and very approachable. You will probably be the same way when you're in that position in the near future.

To be most efficient, you only want to approach the people who bid because there will also be people there that don't have money who are just watching. Your message will be the same, "Hey, I saw that you bid on (address of property) in there. My name is _____. I'm a local real estate investor as well. Sometimes I come across discount properties that I can't always fund with my own cash, so I am looking to grow a network of other investors that I can send deals to when I get them if I can't fund them. Are you okay with me sending you deals I come across? Great…(get their info).

Just as a tip: If you have a ton of buyers at one sale, you may not be able to have a detailed discussion with all of them. Sometimes it's better just to meet them, ask their name, and see if they have a business card, or friend them later on Facebook or LinkedIn. You can always message them later with your proposition.

First of all, you want to attend the actual live auctions to network with Cash Buyers. But, even more importantly, you want to learn how the and when the county publishes "Notice of Defaults". A notice of default is when someone doesn't pay their mortgage. The mortgage company then files a notice of default which starts the foreclosure process. Notice of defaults are public information. Your local county will have public records of people that have just been served with a notice of default.

Getting a list of people who have been issued a notice of default gives you a list of potentially Motivated Sellers to add to your list. If they haven't paid their mortgage, there is a reason. Did they lose their job? Financial hard times? Going through divorce? You could potentially help these people out of a bad situation by offering to take over their mortgage payments or giving them a cash offer without the red tape that they will experience with traditional banks. And your offer can get them out from under their situation quick.

What you want to do is get a list of people who have JUST been issued a notice of default. Some counties have this information published online, which makes it easy. But some make you read the paper or publish it on a paper at the courthouse. Whatever the process is, you need to learn it. And as soon as someone is given a notice of default, you want to know, so you can put them on your list of potentially Motivated Sellers.

Once you figure out where to get a list of pre-foreclosures to your county, look for the ones who have a foreclosure date that is set out the farthest. You will have the best opportunity to save these people from going to foreclosure. That being said, you want to visit ALL of them. You could end up getting a cash partner in just a few days based off your previous efforts. When you have a Cash Buyer, you can tell him about a house that is going to auction, and possibly partner on it.

The next thing you are going to do at the courthouse, is learn how the tax liens are handled in your county. People who have tax liens are people who haven't paid their property taxes on a house that they own in the county. People who haven't found a way to pay their property taxes actually make for a great source of potentially Motivated Sellers. What you will want to do is find out where you can find the publication of all the properties that were in last years AND this upcoming year's tax lien sales. This is all public information so don't feel like you are doing anything nefarious here. Typically, what your county will publish is the parcel number and the lien amount.

County employees are filled with a kind of people I call "Flo". Flo is typically incredibly very helpful. So just find your local Flo that works in the county office and oversees the tax lien process, and ask her how you can find out from the parcel number, what the address of the property is, and who owns it, so you can send them a letter in the mail to see if you can help them out of a potential "motivated to sell" situation.

Add these people to your Motivated Seller list. Name and address may be all you need to start. But you can also cross reference names with Facebook to see if you might be able to privately message them as well. Just as a side note here: some people might think looking them up on Facebook is an extreme measure....

Let me just take this opportunity to give a motivational speech here. You might just want to do what's "comfortable". That's fine. Your money zone will be your comfort zone. If you want to get a cubicle prison (I mean job) working 40 plus hours a week for $44,000 a year, with the promise of a gold watch when you retire at 79, then do what's comfortable and never step outside your comfort zone. But we don't have time and we don't have the money to be comfortable here. If we want to be successful we need to do the things that nobody else is comfortable doing or that nobody else even THINKS of doing. It's not that hard, actually. Just send them a message on Facebook. I PROMISE you......nobody else is. And you very easily could uncover a deal that a BILLION DOLLAR real estate company out of New York or L.A. couldn't uncover with their million-dollar post card advertising campaign. You're David, and they're Goliath. And YOU, my friend, have a rock and sling and they have no idea what's coming.

End motivational speech rant.

Find out how the parcel number can give you the name, number, and address of the owner who is having trouble paying their tax liens, and then do whatever it takes to get in touch with that person.

Next item on the agenda for the courthouse visit: You want to learn how the probate process works and how you can contact someone who is in charge of an inherited property. Probate is the process of distributing the property of a deceased person. You want to find your Flo at your local courthouse and figure out how you can contact people who are in charge or have just been assigned as the executors of inherited property. Again, you're not doing anything sneaky here. This is all public record.

Not everyone, but some people who have inherited property don't want that property. They have just had a loved one die. What's worse is that they don't have time or money to upkeep their inherited property. They also don't have time or money to pay the property taxes or mortgage on that property or take care of the items inside. Your opportunity here is to take this property off their hands while solving their problem with the stuff inside the property. More on that later.

Right now, your goal is to get a list of people that are in charge of inherited property and how you can contact them so that you can discuss how you can help solve their potential problems. Flo can help you with that. Make sure to say please and thank you and give her a gift card to Outback Steak House. This will pay DIVIDENDS in the future!

3pm-5pm Put a Line in the Water for Potential Owner Financed Buyers-

Now it's time to grow your list of Owner Finance Buyers- These are people who might give you a down payment for a home that you own. So create another tab on a spreadsheet or notebook for your Owner Financed Buyer database. You will contact them as soon as you get an owner financed deal under contract. Here is what it should look like:

	A	B	C	D	E
1	Name	Have a cash for a down payment?	Does credit need to be improved?	Type of house they are looking for?	What are they able to pay monthly?
2					
3					
4					

Your goal is to fill this database up with as many potential Owner Financed Buyer as possible.

We're going to do this in two places right now: Facebook and Craigslist.

Let's focus on Facebook first. Search for real estate groups and clubs in your area on Facebook. Join them and start providing valuable interaction with people on the group first. Don't come right out and start soliciting people. That's how you get kicked out of a group right away. Provide some value first. Then what you want to do is use the polling feature on Facebook or just ask a question to get responses below.

Simply post, "Question for everyone: how many of you currently rent, but would love to become a homeowner if you found the right owner financed deal that helped you grow your wealth every month?" This typically gets some really good responses.

When people respond, you want to privately message them something like, "Hey, I just saw that you said _____ to my question. I'm a real estate investor. One of the things that I do is that I help people become home owners by financing to them the homes that I get. With the banks, you may need great credit and 20% down payment. With me, there is no red tape, and I require a down payment between 5% and 15%, it just depends on the deal. And then I credit your lease monthly towards the purchase price, so you're not throwing your money away on rent. Would you be interested in a deal like that?"

9 times out of 10 they say yes. From there you want to ask them a few more qualifying questions and get them on your spreadsheet:

Great! Could you come up with some kind of down payment, depending on how much it was?...Does credit need to be improved? It's ok if it does, that's part of what we help people with.... What kind of house would you be interested in? Bed? Bathrooms? Square footage?....What is your monthly price range?....Another good question after they give you the price range is... if I get a deal that is beyond that price range, would you still like me to send it to you, or do you only want to look at things in that range?

Then add them to your database. At this point, you should be having all the lines in the water that you need that will help you start creating those 3 databases. Databases of potential Motivated Sellers, Cash Buyers, and Owner Financed Buyers.

The worst thing that can possibly happen from here is that you don't check your nets to see what kind of fish you bring in. It's one thing to set the trap, it's another to check it to see if you caught anything. Make sure from here that you are responding and qualifying all of the leads you get in from Facebook and Craigslist.

5pm- Reflect on the day-

Give yourself a pat on the back. You had a great day! You accomplished a lot. You set your lines. You got hands on experience with the right strategy. You're doing all the things you need to do in order to get $10k in the next 29 days. Make sure to end your day with gratitude. Personally, I like to reflect on 4 questions:

Did I do everything in my control to hit my goals today? If not—what do I need to focus on improving tomorrow?
Did I learn something new?
Did I do something outside my comfort zone?
What was my area of genius today?

DAY 2

Ready...Fire...Aim

5am-5:30am- **Wake up, Coffee, and Prayer/Meditation.**

Today is going to be awesome, but you will need to challenge yourself to get outside your comfort zone. You will need to have courage. Here is a great quote from a motivational speaker named Elliott Hulse. You can chew on this for your reflection today. You can find this on YouTube, from a Goalcast video as well, but here is the transcription below:

"Do the thing you're afraid to do. DO IT! It's not about feeling confident about going into the situation. It's not about knowing that it's going to work out. It's not about having the most detailed plan for how this thing will happen, it's about doing it. Courage.

Courage is what you will experience and what you will grow when the doubt is there, but you do it anyway. Your problem isn't doubt. Your problem is courage. Doubt is going to be there, but doubt gets out of the way when you express courage. Doubt is burned off by courage.

Ralph Waldo Emerson said, 'Do the thing and you will have the power.' We're waiting, waiting, waiting for the power. We're waiting not to self-doubt any longer. Whatever it is that you're deciding that you want to do with yourself, that you're doubting your ability on, just do it. F#ck it up completely.

That's another thing that you got to get through your mind, is that success is not doing the right thing and it definitely isn't doing the right thing the first time. Success is having the courage to move in the direction of your dreams. Move in the direction that your heart is taking you. That is what success is, as you are progressively realizing that thing.

People think success is, 'I've got a plan and I'm going to work out that plan.' It never, ever, ever, ever, ever works that way. Success is the progressive realization of a worthy goal, but progressive realization means that you're doing things that you don't know how to do. You're stepping out in faith. You are being courageous. Your self-doubt will step out of the way when you build the balls to do the thing."

That is a GREAT message for what you will do today! After you're done reflecting on that, reflect on this line right here, "It's a numbers game. Even a blind squirrel will find a nut".

And, "Your bank account will grow with your comfort zone."

5:30am-6:00am- Exercise and Stretch-

Today's theme is to really push yourself. Push yourself in your workout and you'll push yourself throughout the day as well. So whatever your work out is for today, push yourself a little more than normal.

6:00am-6:30am- Plan Your Drive for Dollars

You made lists yesterday. There are people you can call and talk to, and there are addresses that you can visit. Because we only have limited time, we're going to start with visiting addresses. Why?

Because you end up getting new leads every time you go drive for dollars. You will see grass that's overgrown. This could be a Motivated Seller. You will see a house with a "for sale by owner" sign in it. This could be a Motivated Seller. Some of the best deals I've gotten as well, didn't come from calling someone on the phone. It came from making a personal visit.

At this time, you want to take all the addresses of people going through foreclosure that you got yesterday when you went to the courthouse. Start creating a driving map to visit each and every person on your list, starting with the ones who are the farthest out from foreclosure.

Next, you will take your tax lien sale list and you will create a driving map for these people as well. But note that, the way you talk to someone going through a tax lien will be different from the way you talk to someone going through pre-foreclosure. We'll go over that in just a second.

What I like doing when mapping out driving for dollars is using a multi route planner and optimization tool on map quest. You can get the multi route planner here: https://www.mapquest.com/routeplanner

That way, you don't have to back track. You can just go through all of your addresses in the most efficient way possible.

6:30am-8:00am- Strategize and Visualize

There are two ways to go about driving for dollars. You can actually knock on every single door and talk to each person, OR you can leave a note. I prefer a combination of both. Do whatever you know you will do. Your money zone will be your comfort zone, so remember that. That being said, if the thought of knocking on someone's door and talking to them is so scary to you that you just won't do it, then just post a note on the door, asking them to call you. It's better to do something than to do nothing.

You will want to use the post-it note strategy. When I first started working the pre-foreclosure market, and I would speak to these people or I would get to walk in their house, there is one thing you will notice right away. And this is that they have a stack of mail about as high as the ceiling. The big real estate companies and wholesalers are budgeting marketing dollars to send mailers to these people. It can be effective, but the rate of return is very low on mailers. The reason is: PEOPLE GOING THROUGH FINANCIAL DURESS DON'T OPEN THEIR MAIL.

Put yourself in their shoes. They have creditors chasing them, they have people calling them asking them to pay their bills, and they have just decided to quit answering and quit opening their mail. So you have to do something that really stands out if you want to get their attention.

What I do, is I just get the largest brightest colored post-it note that they sell at the store. They are typically bright orange, pink, yellow, or green. And I will hand write a message on each note and post it on their front door if they don't answer. Or if you are uncomfortable knocking, you can just walk up and post it on the door.

The hand-written message for foreclosure looks something like this:

"Hi <<first name>>, (your pre-foreclosure list probably publishes the name of the person, so I would definitely use it). My name is Ryan and I am a local real estate investor looking in your neighborhood. You had a notice of default that was posted to public records for this house. If this is accurate, I specialize in helping people in situations like yours. There are two things I do that can help your situation. Please feel free to give me a call at 555-555-5555 to discover the opportunity you have with me. Take care,

Ryan"

It's as simple as that. Then I just post it on their door. The bright color gets their attention. And it's personalized so they know they are talking to a real person.

Your message is going to be slightly different for the tax lien list:

"Hi <<first name>>, my name is Ryan and I am a local real estate investor looking for investment property in your neighborhood. I noticed from the public records that there was a tax lien listed for this property. I specialize in helping people in situations like this. If you're interested in seeing how I can help, please give me a call at 555-555-5555 to discover the opportunity you have with me. Take Care,

Ryan"

So what do you do when they call? You want to get as much information about their property as possible. I recommend establishing a relationship first and attempt to empathize with their situation. Sometimes, people like to explain their situation. It's very important to be a good listener.

After you have really understood their situation and their motivation, a good thing to do would be to say something like:

"Well there are two ways I can help with this situation: 1) I can make you a cash offer for your home, or 2) I can structure an owner financed purchase that will improve your credit and hopefully give you a little extra cash as well to move on to the next chapter of your life.

If I could get a little extra information about the property from you, I'll make you both offers and let you know the benefits and you can decide which one you want to pursue.

My goal is to find a situation that is a win for you and is a win for me as an investor as well. In order to do that, I need to have as much info as possible about the property. Can I ask you a few questions about the house?"

This is where you try to get as many numbers as possible to figure out how to structure an offer. There ARE programs out there that you can pay for that will tell you what year they got their mortgage, the interest rate, the monthly payments, etc. I'll include that resource on the resource page. But since we are going through this exercise like we don't have any money, the easiest thing to do is to just ask.

- What are your monthly payments on the house right now?
- How much is the loan payment, and what are the taxes and insurance?
- Are there any other monthly fees associated with the house like HOA dues?
- Do you remember your interest rate?
- Do you know how much is owed on the loan?
- What do you think the house is worth?
- Is there anything that needs to be fixed, repaired, or renovated in the house?
- What is the total square footage?
- How old is it?
- How much money do you owe the mortgage company in back payments? Or/ how much is the tax lien and what is still owed?

After you ask them all of the qualifying questions, the next step is to set up a time for you to view the house tomorrow. In that time in between, you want to be doing your own research on the house and make sure you understand what kind of offer you can make. We'll go over analyzing a deal shortly, so don't worry about that right now.

All you need to know right now, is that later today, you're going to start analyzing the info from this morning and start preparing to make no risk offers tomorrow. Make sure you pull up your database as you go and take notes on who you talked to, what information they were able to give you about the house, and the next steps you need to take so that you can populate your database with the most updated and relevant information.

8:00am- Shop

Go to the store and pick up a post-it note and a thin sharpie to write your post-it messages. Make sure you take your driving for dollars map and list with you and have as much info as you can before speaking to everyone at each address. It is helpful to know the name of the person. You should be able to find the name in the public records.

8:30am- Noon- Go driving for dollars.

When you're hungry, you can do two things: a) You can set lines and traps and wait for food to come to you. Or b) You can grab a bow and arrow, a spear, or a fishing pole and go out and get it. In season 1 of Alone, the winner set traps. In season 2, the winner couldn't catch anything in his traps. All of his food he had to go out and get. But that particular strategy paid off for him.

You already set your nets, traps, and lines yesterday. We don't have time to wait to see what those pull in. You never know which strategy is going to pay off the best for you. So that we cover all bases, we are going with strategy B today. We're going hunting. We're going driving for dollars. You are literally going to hop in your car and drive until you find an opportunity.

You've already planned out your addresses, but don't let this opportunity go to waste. If you see a for sale by owner sign, call on it. If you see grass over grown at a property, take down the address so you can go back to the courthouse later and cross reference the address with a name and see if it is an absentee owner that may be motivated to sell.

A few other tips about driving for dollars. Just get in and get out. Don't be a creep trying to psyche yourself up in the driveway for 15 minutes while all the neighbors wonder what you're doing. Be confident. Like the reflection for today said, "do the thing!"

Also, you're a real estate investor. Don't be too shy to let anyone know. You are not doing anything illegal here. You are a real estate investor potentially interested in investing in various neighborhoods. Don't be afraid to talk to the neighbors. When I first started, it was not uncommon for me to go post a note on someone's door who did not answer it, and then go talk to a neighbor that I saw outside.

There are multiple benefits to talking with the neighbors:

- A neighbor may know of a way to contact the person that you don't.
- A neighbor can give you the motivation of the person looking to sell and their backstory which could help in negotiations.
- A neighbor can let you know who the original builder of the house was, and if there has ever been anything wrong with it. One time, I got a $230,000 house at the foreclosure sale for only $134,000 because I talked to a neighbor who told me the previous owners did a test to see if there was any Chinese drywall and there wasn't. No other investors invested because they weren't sure if it had Chinese drywall or not. I had that piece of knowledge from talking to a neighbor and got a house almost $100,000 under value. Talking to neighbors pays.
- A neighbor sometimes knows other people who need to sell their house fast and may give you another lead.

Bottom line, as you go through this exercise, you will make more money if you develop as many positive relationships as possible. And those relationships include neighbors of distressed homes.

Last thing about driving for dollars: don't waste your time in the car. There is one thing that will get you from point A to point B the fastest- and that is knowledge. When I first got started, as I went driving for dollars, I listened to audio books, podcasts, YouTube videos, courses that I purchased, and all kind of other sources to learn how to do certain things. Make sure you have some knowledge ready for your drive. If you're looking for recommendations (ahem…shameless plug) you can start with the Cash Flow Dad Life podcast, the CashFlow DadLife YouTube videos, and the free web training video that I have for you that shows you exactly "How I Made $387,000 in Passive Income in Less Than 12 Months….Using Under the Radar Real Estate Investing Secrets…With Hardly Any Money To My Name and With 0 Experience". There is a link for this training on your resource page.

Noon-2pm. (or while you're driving)- Find a Good Divorce Attorney, Marriage Counselor, and Bankruptcy Attorney in the Area

When you don't have something, you start looking around to see who's got what you need. And maybe you have something they need. If you can help them, then they will be inclined to help you.

The more people you are able to help, the faster the help will come back to you. As you are going around talking to people who weren't able to pay their mortgage, or weren't able to pay their tax lien, you will notice that some of them need help and don't know what to do next.

You are going to help them, for free, **EVEN IF IT MEANS THAT YOU LOSE THAT PARTICULAR DEAL**. That's right, you read that correctly, and I put it in bold and all caps, so it stood out. What you need to realize, is that the world has a way of returning favors. If you go into today thinking that you are going to be a shark preying on weak people, you will fail. You are going to go out and find as many people as possible to help. Money will follow you if your intention is to help and solve problems.

First, you are going to go onto Google and search "divorce attorney (your city)". "marriage counselor (your city)", "bankruptcy attorney (your city)". Try to get at least 5 people in each category and call them all. You are looking for someone to be on your team here that you can refer business to. The conversation looks like this:

"Hi, my name is Ryan, I am a real estate investor in this area. I come across a lot of people that are starting the process of foreclosure and many of them need a good bankruptcy attorney. So I am just looking for a good bankruptcy attorney to refer them to. Do you help people in these situations? ....Is it ok if I start referring people to you?"

Same for the marriage counselor or divorce attorney:

"Hi my name is Ryan, I am a real estate investor in this area. Many people I come across that I am able to help are going through relationship problems or the beginning stages of divorce. How can you help people like this and is it ok if I start referring people to you?"

Here's the key here: it's called the Principle of Reciprocity. When you open the door for someone else, by the laws of human nature they want to turn around and help you out. As you talk to people going through foreclosure, if they say they are having spousal problems, recommend either the counselor or divorce attorney (use your judgment here). If they are going through financial duress, you can recommend the bankruptcy attorney. Give the owner of the house their name and number and tell them to make sure to mention that they heard about them from you.

So right now, do a search and call on some bankruptcy attorneys, marriage counselors, and divorce attorneys. And pick which one in each category you are going to refer your people to. Your currency is not just telling them you are going to start referring people to them, it's to actually bring them a referral.

After you bring them a referral, it's appropriate to say, "Did (name) call you? I gave him your number. He did? Great! Hope you are able to work something out with him and give him some peace about his situation. Hey listen, if you come across anyone as well that I may be able to help as a real estate investor, feel free to send them over to me."

….See what you just did there? You set another line. This networking will pay off long term. Eventually, you will get to the point where you don't have to go out looking for deals. They just come to you because you set up these relationships correctly.

3pm-5pm- Analyze the Potential Value of the Properties

You will want to get advanced training on this later, but time is of the essence, so here is what we are going to do right now to analyze the deal:

Go to Zillow.com and type in the address. Zillow is not 100% accurate, but they seem to be getting better as time goes by with their algorithms. They are way more accurate now than they were, even 6 months ago. So when you go to Zillow and type in the address, they are going to have something they call a "zestimate" which is their estimate on how much the house is worth.

Find 3 other sold properties in the area that have been sold in the last 6 months in the same neighborhood. Just click on the Zillow map near the property and click on the criteria and click "sold". For each property that is comparable, write down the square footage and what the property was sold for. The number you are trying to arrive at is the sold price per square foot. To get this number you divide the sale price by the square footage of the property. For example, if a house sells for $200,000 and it has 2000 square feet. The sold price per square foot is $200,000 divided by 2000, equaling $100 a square foot.

Take the average of the 3 sold properties sold price per square foot. So say it's, $100 per square foot for the first one, $120 for the second one, and $90 for the third one. The average of those 3 sold prices is $100 plus $120 plus $90 divided by 3, equaling $103.33.

Multiply the average sold price per square foot by the square footage of the house you are looking at. So, say the house you are looking at is 2100 square feet. That means it is probably worth around $216,993 (2100 x $103.33).

If you want to cross reference this price call a real estate brokerage firm and ask them for what's known as a BPO (broker price opinion). You will want to network with a realtor anyways. This will be free for you as realtors work on commission. This is what that conversation might look like:

"Hey (realtor name), my name is Ryan, and I am a real estate investor in the area. I'm calling for two reasons: 1) I'm currently looking for a realtor that is good with working with investors. I'm on the hunt for investment property and I wanted to see if you had any opportunities you might be able to send me. 2) I have a property that I just found, and I wanted to see if you wouldn't mind giving me your opinion of what it is worth, so I can make an offer."

A good and hungry realtor will do this for free because they work for straight commission. When I was a realtor I did stuff like this for free all the time in the hopes that I could generate some business for myself down the road. Working with an investor is way better than working with individuals, because investors buy multiple properties. Their relationship with you could be a steady stream of income for them down the road. So don't feel bad for trying to get something for free from a realtor. If they are good, you will likely kick some business their way down the road.

Once you have a pretty good idea of what the price per square foot is in the area, you will want to back out any of the costs of renovations. You may or may not have seen the properties inside at this point as you are driving around. More than likely, you have all your appointments to view property setup for tomorrow. So just be aware, that while looking through the house, you are going to want to take a note of any renovations you may need to make in order to get the house to that average sold price per square foot value.

Right now, you are just looking at ONE NUMBER. How much would the house be worth, if it didn't need any renovations. After going through the steps above, you should have a pretty good idea.

5pm-5:15pm- Check your nets

Yesterday you put out a few lines, traps, and nets to bring in Motivated Sellers, Cash Buyers, and Owner Financed Buyers. Check your email, texts, and voicemail and make sure you get back to everyone. This seems so obvious, but this can often times be overlooked. You can sometimes get a ton of messages. Some of them are what I call "wasters". People that waste your time. You might have to sift through some wasters before you get a really good opportunity. But don't let a few wasters discourage you from calling people back. Talk to everyone. You never know what kind of opportunity you might get from it.

5:15pm-6pm- Reflect on your day with gratitude

Man! You're crushing it! You have accomplished so much in just 2 days. Not only are you discovering opportunities immediately, but also, you're setting your networks up for the long run. You've learned how to uncover deals. You've gotten experience talking to Motivated Sellers. Maybe you didn't say all the right things. That's ok. You probably have a great idea on how to say it better tomorrow. ***We're looking for progress, not perfection.***

Most importantly, you've started to fill your lists with all kinds of potential deals, and you have some appointments set up for tomorrow. Today has been an amazing day.

Time to reflect once again:
- Did I do everything in my control to hit my goals today? If not—what do I need to focus on improving tomorrow?
- Did I learn something new?
- Did I do something outside my comfort zone?
- What was my area of genius today?

DAY 3
Trust the Blueprint

5:00am-5:30am-Wake up/Coffee/Prayer/Meditation-

Today we are going to focus on the blueprint and trusting the blueprint. You now have 2 days under your belt. If you followed the blueprint, you're going to have a tremendous amount of breakthrough and success in just two days. If you didn't follow the blueprint, you might be wondering right now if it works.

There's a phrase they use in 12 step programs. 12 step programs are programs that addicts go to in order to change bad habits in their life. The problem is that many of these addicts have patterns of quitting the program too soon, of giving up or despairing the first time something doesn't work. And to make matters worse, they are surrounding themselves with the wrong people that are trying to pull them back into their past destructive situations and patterns. So they invented a phrase for addicts to say to themselves every time they get discouraged going through the 12 steps. And that phrase is, "It works if you work it. So work it...it's worth it."

If you are trying to change your life and create new habits, and you've got 30 days to do it, this blueprint to make 10k in less than a month with Real Estate Investing works. You just have to work it. So at this point, if you haven't taken action on the steps above, you are probably struggling with self-doubt, insecurity, doubt with the system, or you are surrounded by other discouraging people. If you're at that point now, don't panic, and definitely DON'T QUIT. Let's fuel your mind right now with what you need to overcome that obstacle, so we can make this day one of our best yet!

This is an excerpt from an interview with John Assaraf. If you don't know who John is, he is the author of the book "The Secret", and owner of multi-million dollar companies that include real estate, software, brain research, and life/business coaching. But he started out as a poor street thug in Israel, who wasn't good at anything but getting in trouble. You can find the full clip on the YouTube channel "Motivation Addicts". But here is the excerpt to chew on today:

"Show me who your friends are and I'll tell you who YOU are. When I was a kid, I had a lot of my own challenges. I didn't have a whole lot of confidence in myself. I didn't believe in myself. I had some big challenges with the law. Getting in trouble in school. Getting in trouble outside of school.

And I was really fortunate when I was 19 years old. I met a wonderful gentleman who was very successful with his family. He was very successful with giving to charities. He was very healthy, he was very gentle and kind, and he really wanted to do good in the world. Not just for himself, but to make the world a better place. And he started to teach me that the reason I was getting into trouble.

The reason I wasn't getting great results was what I believed about myself. And he taught me the power of my beliefs. He taught me the power of what I do every single day matters. He taught me the power of the intelligence in the universe. That I could utilize my brain like a radio sends a signal out into the universe using the power of your thoughts. You are also capable of receiving information just like the great inventors, whether it was Albert Einstein, whether it was Edison, whether it was Michael Angelo: Any of the great inventors that had these ideas that just came to them. And they were just normal human beings, but they took advantage of the messages that they were getting in their hearts and their intuition.

And so, he taught me the power of the brain and by using what I learned, I learned that I could achieve a lot more than I ever thought was possible when I was younger. And so now I want to take what I learned for 33 years and teach it to other people to make the path for them a little bit easier.

Yeah, I was getting into a lot of trouble. I was doing some very dangerous things that I could have died or gone to jail for. And when he started to share with me and teach me that my entire reality was what I believed was real, what was true about myself and what I thought was possible, and that I could change that, that's when my life started to change.

If you start to change the way you think, AND you start to learn every day for one hour to upgrade your KNOWLEDGE and your SKILLS, and then you TAKE ACTION every day on the things that are the most important, instead of all the different things that you can do. He said if you can focus on doing 3 to 5 things every day towards your goals he said in one year, you will be in a totally different destination. Three years, BIG distinction, five to ten years, your life won't be the same.

And I was tired of living a mediocre to less than mediocre life. So I said, 'Listen, you seem to have a good plan and a good path. You're making millions of dollars.

You're giving a lot of money to charity. You're happy. You're healthy. You've got a great family. I want THAT.'

He said that if you want that, follow the blueprint. Don't try to figure it out. Just follow the blueprint. And that was another lesson that he shared with me. You don't have to reinvent the wheel. Like if you want to fly right now, you don't need to figure out how to fly. There's already a blueprint for how to generate or create an airplane. If you want to be healthy, there is already a blueprint. If you want to make more money, there's already a blueprint. If you want to buy real estate, or the stock market, or start a business or grow a business, there are people before us that have already got the blueprint. All you have to do is paint the numbers inside the box. And then you can use your creativity.

So I just became a very good follower for a long time of things that worked. And when you follow things that work, it's like being given the combination to a safe. If someone gives you a combination to a safe, and they tell you to turn this way a little bit, and then this way a little bit, and then turn this way a little bit, then open it, you can have access to it. But most people don't look for the combination. And then even when they get the combination, they try it in the wrong order.

And so I learned at a very young age to at least follow the initial plans. Then, if you want to get creative, you can add your creativity and your genius to that as well."

Remember as you're going through today to just follow the blueprint. It works if you work it. So work it....it's worth it. Take a few minutes to really let this sink in.

5:30am- 6:00am- Set Goals and Visualize Your Success with Them

Today, we are going to do several things:
- Visit people we made appointments with. You should already have appointments set up to see some houses. And you very likely have set up a meeting with potential cash buyers to take them out for coffee, lunch, or beer. I call these CLB meetings. It's the best way to get investors.
- You will continue to "check your traps" and set up appointments
- You will learn how to inspect a house and estimate repairs
- You will execute your call lists from day 1 that you didn't visit on day 2.
- You will add a new player on your team that can help you execute owner financed deals and wholesale deals.

6am-6:30am- Map out your drive and make sure you know where you are going and at what time you are going to be there. Now is also a good time to plan on what kind of knowledge you are going to soak up on your drive (ahem…cashflowdadlife podcast, YouTube channel, webinar, supplemental training).

6:30am-7:30am- Learn the skill of how to inspect a house

Go to YouTube and research how to inspect a house. Just search "how to inspect a house" and there are a ton of videos that come up. You are going to be visiting some houses today, and it would be good for you to know what to look for. Just so you fully understand the purpose of learning this and how to apply it: you're not going to perform a full inspection on any house today. That is what the inspection period is for. But you do want to be able to walk through a house and eye things up. Tinker with an AC unit here. Flip a breaker there. Just so the owner knows you have knowledge of houses.

7:30am- 8:30am- Learn how to cost out renovations in your area

As you are going through these houses, you may notice that they need some improvement. If you are going to keep the house yourself, you can't have something that is going to take more than 30 days to fix. So keep that in mind. If you find a house like that, you still want to get it under contract if it's a deal. But you are definitely going to want to wholesale it.

Whether or not you are wholesaling the deal, or keeping it for yourself, you will want to price out how much renovations might cost, and factor that cost into your offer. There is a really cool resource you can use for this. It's called homewyse.com. They basically collect data from different zip codes from Home Depot and Lowes and what not, and they give you a price range on how much any particular project would cost.

If you go into a house, and you see that the floors need to be replaced, and you think hardwood floors would look great in that house. You can just go to homewyse.com, plug in the square footage and your zip code, and they will shoot out to you an estimate on how much it should cost for materials and labor in your area. Here's an example of what homewyse will show you:

Cost to Install a Hardwood Floor
Updated: March 2018

Hardwood Floor Installation Calculator		Zip Code 47474	Square Feet* 120		Update
Item details		Qty		Low	High
☑ **Hardwood Flooring Cost** Non-discounted retail pricing for: Residential, above-grade red oak flooring. 25 yr limited warranty. UV resistant 7 coat AIO satin finish. For nail down installation. Quantity includes typical waste overage, material for repair and local delivery.		129 SF		$432	$568
☑ **Hardwood Flooring Labor, Basic** Basic labor to install hardwood floor with favorable site conditions. Install underlayment on clean, level subfloor. Acclimate, cull and blend flooring. Blind nail wood flooring. Includes planning, equipment and material acquisition, area preparation and protection, setup and cleanup.		7.0 h		$439	$713
☑ **Hardwood Flooring Job Supplies** Cost of related materials and supplies typically required to install hardwood floor including: manufacturer recommended underlayment, fasteners, adhesives and surface sealants.		129 SF		$55	$62
☑ **Hardwood Flooring Equipment Allowance** Job related costs of specialty equipment used for job quality and efficiency, including: Pneumatic nailer for 1 1/2" to 2" nails and up to 3/4" thick flooring. Daily rental. Consumables extra.		1 job		$38	$56
☐ **Option: Remove Flooring** Detach from mounting surface(s). Break into haul able pieces. Remove from home and dispose of legally. Asbestos handling is extra.		6.1 h		$307	$618
☐ **Hardwood Flooring Debris Disposal** Costs to load and haul away old materials, installation waste and associated debris.		120 SF		$28	$32
Totals - Cost To Install Hardwood Floor		120 SF		**$963**	**$1,399**
Average Cost per Square Foot				**$8.03**	**$11.66**

Customize & Print Job Estimates

It's pretty awesome. And specifically, since we are trying to move forward on a shoestring budget, it's really cool that it's 100% FREE. It's going to show you on the low side what you can expect to pay for materials and labor, and what you can expect on the high side. So just spend this time messing with it and looking at what different renovations and costs might be in your area. Start with 1000 square feet as an estimate. That way if you're talking to a motivated seller and you guys acknowledge that you would need to put in new floors, you can just throw out there, "yeah, ok, it's gonna be about $10 a square foot for floors. So at

1000 square feet, we're looking at about $10k in renovations."

Making comments like this helps to pre-frame any kind of offer you may make. It sets the expectation right out of the gate that they may not get the ask price for the house. The trick is just to be very polite about any renovations or costs that might come up while you are viewing the house. Some people are emotionally attached to the house and you do NOT want to insult them.

8:30am-9:30am- Find Your Secret Weapon

In the show, Alone, everyone could bring whatever tools they wanted to bring in order to survive. People brought all kinds of different stuff. But one tool that every single person on the show brought, was the fire starter flint stick. Because without the flint stick, it would be very difficult to make a fire, especially with the wet wood that they had. Without a fire, it would be very difficult to eat all the food at their disposal and stay warm in the winter. And without food and warmth...well...

In real estate, our fire starter is the Title Attorney who knows how to execute creatively financed deals. Without the title attorney, we're dead in the water. We can't wholesale a contract by double closing or contract assignment. We can't do a mortgage take over or lease option. And we won't have anyone that can customize our contracts to fit local law.

Real quick note on this: Similar to the real estate agent, if you find the right title attorney, they will customize your contract for free as long as they are confident that you will close future deals with them. They make the money with the closings.

Do a search on google with "Title Company Wholesaling", "Title Company Owner Financing", or "Title Company Creative Financing". You want to find at least 3 to 5 title companies that will do this. A title company name may not come up in a search right away that is specifically geared to wholesaling. That's ok. Many title companies don't specialize in it, but they know how to do it. Preferably you find someone that specializes, but if not, you can just find someone that knows how to execute it. So at this point, give all the companies a call and your conversation should look something like this:

Receptionist: Company Name Title, how can I help you?

You: Yes, I am a real estate investor, and I have some deals pending that I am considering wholesaling. I am looking for a good title company that is familiar with this process: Either with double closings or contract assignments. Do you guys do this?

If the receptionist answers no, then move on. If she answers yes, you will want to ask some supplemental questions:

Which method do you find most effective or are you most familiar with? Double Closing? Or Contract Assigning? Do you have a recommended contract that I should use? Once I have a contract in hand, what process do you recommend I go through with your title company?

Even if you find a good title company on the first phone call that will do this, I would still recommend calling a few others. What you really want is to get a hold of someone that you like, and that is incredibly helpful and willing to share their knowledge with you. So just call a few places to see which one you think will be the most helpful to you.

Real Estate processes and laws are different in different states and even in different counties and cities. This title company will help to make sure, however, that you do this the legit way. Where I live, my title company actually doesn't call it a double closing and they don't call it a contract assignment. He doesn't even have a name for the process, but he knows how to make it work. I don't care. I can't be worried about what it's called. And you shouldn't worry either. All you need to focus on is finding that good title attorney who knows how the process works and can explain to you what you need to do to execute the process.

Commit that process to memory and be confident when you talk to cash buyers on how you are going to execute the deal.

9:30am-11:30am- Execute Your Call List for Motivated Sellers and Setup Appointments to View the Property

Remember that real estate is a numbers game. The more people you call, the more deals you will get. Let's talk about how these different conversations should sound based on the type of person you are calling. When you're going fishing, you don't use the same bait for every fish. If you're fishing for catfish, you want to fish off the bottom without a bobber and with some bait that really stinks. If you're fishing for trout, depending on the season, you want to use a bobber, and you may want to use a lure instead of live bait if you know how to move the line right.

Real estate is the same way. You will have different conversations based on different types of people that you talk to. Let's go first to all the people on your potential motivated sellers list. And let's start with people who advertised their house for rent.

Send them a text message that says, "Hey, my name is (Ryan). I saw on Craigslist that you have (X) property available for rent. I'm an investor and I'm actually looking for investment property in this area. Would consider selling?"

For some reason, I have found the text message to be more effective for landlords. Mostly because it is a less threatening and efficient way to have the conversation with someone who hasn't listed their property with the purpose you are contacting them.

What do we have here if they say "yes"? We have a potential "Owner Financed" deal. You already know that they are willing to take just a monthly payment for the property. So all you have to do is find a situation that works for them where they can owner finance it to you. The main benefit to them, is that they have an exit strategy on the property, and they no longer have to take care of any of the maintenance issues or tenant headaches on the house.

If they say yes, the next thing you will want to do is analyze the deal. Go through that process of figuring out what the house is worth. But you also want to see what a good market rate is for rent for the property.

So go to Zillow.com. Zillow will have a rent estimate for the area. Cross reference that with other properties that are available to rent in that area on Craigslist.

What your end game will be is to do a lease option contract with them where you have the purchase price at least $10,000 under what it should be valued. And you have a monthly rent payment AT LEAST $100 under what it should be valued. So for example, if it is a house that is worth $150,000 and can get $1300 in rent, you want to see if you can set up the lease option contract for you to purchase the house for at maximum $140,000 and at maximum $1200 a month in rent.

What you will do from here is start marketing the house on Zillow, Craigslist and Facebook marketplace, and go to your owner financed buyers list, and sell it to someone for $10,000 down, and $1300 a month in rent. BOOM! 10k in less than 30 days! Plus, long term passive income cash flow. You're a genius!

If you haven't gotten my lease option contract and training yet, check out the link on the resource page on the back of this book on how to use this contract and for a copy of it. You will want to give it to your title attorney at some point and have him or her make sure that the contract is functional in your locality. Again, if you established a good relationship with the title attorney, it shouldn't cost you anything for them to review it real quick to make sure it's legit.

So, back to your conversation with the guy who said YES, he is willing to sell his rental property. Your next objective will be to set up an appointment for later today if you have time, or for tomorrow to view the property. Don't start negotiating an owner financed deal until you have had a chance to establish a relationship with the guy. Here are some questions you may ask:

- Have you considered what you would sell it for?
- What is the condition of the property?
- Square footage?
- Do you still have a mortgage on it? (this will demonstrate how much wiggle room there is in monthly rents)
- How long have you owned the property?
- When can I take a look at it?

Next, we're going to start calling on everyone else who is a potential motivated seller. Here is how the conversation should go and what kind of questions you should ask them:

"Hey, my name is Ryan. I'm a local real estate investor. I noticed your advertisement that you are selling your property at (address). Can you tell me a little bit about the property?"

"On the advertisement, you said that you were (say the key word you searched for that indicated they could be a Motivated Seller) "motivated/looking to sell fast/ looking for someone to make an offer fast". Can you tell me why you advertised it that way?"

At this point they may start disclosing their motivation. You're going to come back to this. But you want to just ask some general questions about the house and fill out your spreadsheet.

"Are there any renovations needed?"

"What is the square footage of the house?"

"Are there any appliances like the AC or dishwasher that need to be upgraded?"

"What is the age of the house?"

"What is the age of the roof?"

After you're done asking them a few questions about the property, since they are trying to sell it, they will likely be trying to sell you on its best features. Nobody ever lists their house for sale and says, "the AC constantly goes out, I don't know what's wrong with the toilet upstairs, and the neighbor across the street is weird." They're going to say it's a beautiful house, the living room is spacious, and it's got a neighborhood pool.

For whatever reason, most of the time when you ask someone a second time what their motivation is, they tend to give you a more detailed or different answer. So here is what I like to ask the second time,

"Ok, it sounds pretty nice and it may be what I'm looking for. Remind me again...why are you looking to sell?"

After you get the motivation, see if you can set up an appointment to see the house later this afternoon or tomorrow. One thing to note here: if their motivation is pretty clear, they seem pretty desperate, and you have good reason to believe that they would be happy if they could be done with the house in a week if they were able, it would be completely ok to ask one final question to start priming the negotiations.

"Well like I said earlier. I'm a real estate investor. So part of what I do is look for people that I can help out of there situation, and at the same time, structure a deal that I can make money on as well. What is the lowest possible price that you'd be willing to accept on the house if I could get you out of it within a week?"

You may be able to go straight to the house with a contract in hand.

11:30am-12:00pm- Check your lines and see if there are any Cash Buyers, Motivated Sellers, or Owner Financed Buyers in your inbox that you can call.

At this point, you just want to start calling people as they come in and see if you can qualify the opportunity over the phone and set up an appointment. You also may need to "reset your lines". Craigslist for example will fade you out to later dates. You will want to renew all of your posts so you remain at the top of local searches. Same thing with the other places you advertised. Renew or repost so that you can stay in front of opportunities.

12:00pm-1pm- Look at your appointments to see houses today and get an idea of how much you might offer them in "cash".

The worst thing that happened to any of the contestants on the show, "Alone", was that they saw some food, but they were unable to catch it because they didn't have the right equipment prepared at the time. What could be worse than being starving, seeing a fresh salmon swimming upstream, and not having a fishing pole?

It is not uncommon that during your visit you may come across a seller that is so motivated that they would be willing to accept a cash offer right on the spot. You want to be prepared with what you can offer, and you want to be prepared with a purchase agreement. Check out the resource page for how you can get a standard real estate purchase agreement to bring with you for your appointment.

So you already know how to figure out the value of a house. As a rule of thumb, if somebody is motivated, you want to use the **Law of 75%** to make them an offer. This means that if you have a house worth $100,000, you would want to offer them $75,000 minus whatever it may cost to renovate the house.

Why 75%? Because it is common for investor friendly banks to lend someone 75% of the appraised value of a home. What this means to investors is that if they bought a house with all cash at 75% of its appraised value, then they can go back to the bank and take out 100% of the money they put in the house to go buy another house. Buying things at 75% allows them to purchase multiple properties by constantly refinancing a house with a bank. This is an awesome strategy I can teach you later. But right now, what this means to you, is that if you are able to get a house under contract at 75% of its appraised value less the cost of renovations, you are more likely to be able to get a cash buyer that will buy it from you.

What you want to do is a quick appraisal of the value of the home, assuming it is in the condition it is advertised. And then you want to take that value and multiply it by 75%.

Then as you go through the house and estimate repairs if needed, you subtract that cost from the 75%.

Say, for example, you go see a house that you valued at $100,000. This guy is fighting with his wife and is going through a bad divorce and both of them want out yesterday. If you were to make a cash offer it would be $75,000. However, after going through the house you notice that the whole thing needs to be painted in order to have a value of $100,000. The $100,000 is what is known as the After Repair Value or (ARV) in real estate investor speak. So the ARV is $100,000 and the repairs in the form of a paint job are going to cost $4000. You can make a cash offer on the spot for $71,000 ($100,000 *75% minus $4000).

After you have reviewed all potential properties and potential offers you could make on each one based on the 75% rule, you are ready to attend your appointments.

1:00pm- End of Day- Attend your appointments

At this point, you should have a couple of different properties to visit. You may not be able to fit them all in in one day. That's okay, you will have time for appointments tomorrow. You may also have a Coffee Lunch or Beer meeting with a potential investor. This is good, you will already have something you can tell them about and get them excited about the opportunity to invest with you. And perhaps you even have the real estate investment club meeting today or the foreclosure sale is today. You want to make sure to attend all of those events and make the networking contacts you need to make and grow your lists.

As you visit the properties of motivated sellers, make sure to be as polite and confident as possible. The inspection video you watched this morning and messing with renovation prices should help you know what to look for as you go through the house. If you make comments about any repairs that are needed make sure it is polite and doesn't come across as insulting.

At the end of any appointment, if you think you might be able to work something out and make an offer, you want to conclude the appointment by saying something like this:

"Well thank you for your time. I think this might work but I do have a few others that I have set up to look at today. This is strictly a numbers game for me, so I will go home tonight and analyze the numbers and potentially make you an offer that could be a win win for both of us."

5:15pm-6pm- Reflect on the day

Damn this was a great day! You have a couple houses that could make into an amazing deal. You got practice figuring out offer prices. You found an amazing and helpful title attorney who is ready to rock and roll with you. You increased your knowledge on how to look at a house and figure out the cost of renovations. You spoke to some motivated sellers. You got a ton more cash buyers on your list that are ready to pull the trigger with your next deal. You've added to your list of potential Owner Financed Buyers. All you need now, is a house under contract. And you are ready tomorrow to make some offers!

Time to reflect once again:
- Did I do everything in my control to hit my goals today? If not—what do I need to focus on improving tomorrow?
- Did I learn something new?
- Did I do something outside my comfort zone?
- What was my area of genius today?

DAY 4

Staring 14,000 Feet Down from the Top

5:00am-5:30am- Prayer/Reflection/Meditation

Today is the day! Your success with real estate all comes down to what you will do today. And that is to structure and make offers. The person who makes the most offers, wins. If you want 10k or more this week, simply increase the amount of offers that you make. Experts say that for every 18 offers they make, they get 1 deal. So that means that only 5.5% of your offers will go through. It also means, that you only need to make about 18 offers to make some money!

But, there is one HUGE impediment, one fierce enemy to your success here. And that is- fear. The only thing that will prevent you from moving forward and making offers is fear. This morning we are going to reflect deeply on eliminating fear. And we are going to tap into the wisdom of 3 different people here: Will Smith, Jim Carrey, and Jesus.

The actor Will Smith in an interview was asked about his battle with fear, and he shared a story about when he was in Dubai and went skydiving. His story is funny, but his message is a powerful reflection for you on fear:

"Skydiving is a real interesting confrontation with fear. You go out the night before and you take a drink with your friends. And somebody says, 'Yeah! We should go skydiving tomorrow!'

And you say 'Yeah!'

And everybody says 'Yeah!' And everyone is high fiving each other. And then you go home by yourself and you go, 'hmmmmmmmmmm. Right? You know...... like......they was drunk too......'

And that night you're laying in your bed and you're terrified, and you just keep imagining over and over again jumping out of an airplane and you can't figure out why you would do that. So you get there and you have this safety brief. And you're standing there and the guy's going, 'well if the chute doesn't open what's gonna happen...'

And you're like, 'Wait why? What? Why would that happen?'

So you get onto the airplane, and its extra, you know, cause you're sitting on some dude's lap. Some stranger. Trying to make small talk. And you're like, 'Yeah man…so you be jumpin' with people all the time huh?'

So you fly, and you get up to 14,000 feet, and somebody opens the door. And at that moment you realize YOU'VE NEVER BEEN IN A FRICKIN AIRPLANE WITH THE DOOR OPEN. TERROR! TERROR! TERROR! TERROR! And then people start going out of the airplane. And the guy walks you up to the end of the thing. And you're standing. And your toes are on the edge, and you are looking out down to DEATH. They say, 'On 3!..........1!......2!....' And he pushes you on 2 because people grab on 3. And you fall out of the airplane. In 1 second you realize it is THE MOST BLISSFUL EXPERIENCE OF YOUR LIFE. YOU ARE FLYING! There is 0 fear. You realize that **at the point of maximum danger is the point of minimum fear**. The lesson for me was: Why were you scared in your bed the night before? What do you need that fear for? Everything up to the stepping out, there is actually no reason to be scared. And then in that moment, all of sudden, when you are supposed to be terrified is the most blissful experience of your life. And **GOD PLACED THE BEST THINGS IN LIFE ON THE OTHER SIDE OF FEAR.**"

Today, you are going take the action on some things that you may have previously been scared to do. It's important to remember this quote from Will Smith, "The point of maximum danger is the point of minimum fear." And, "God placed the best things in life on the other side of fear." On the other side of your real estate activity is financial freedom to do what you want, when you want, and with who you want. Don't forget that.

In a college graduation speech, the famous comedian and actor, Jim Carrey, gave a very powerful description on how all of our life's decisions come down to a choice between fear and love. Here's what he had to say:

"Fear is going to be a player in your life, but you get to decide how much. You can spend your whole life imagining ghosts, worrying about your pathway to the future, but all there will ever be is what's happening here, and the decisions we make in this moment, which are based in either love or fear.

So many of us choose our path out of fear disguised as practicality. What we really want seems impossibly out of reach and ridiculous to expect, so we never dare to ask the universe for it. I'm saying, I'm the proof that you can ask the universe for it...

My father could have been a great comedian, but he didn't believe that was possible for him, and so he made a conservative choice. Instead, he got a safe job as an accountant, and when I was 12 years old, he was let go from that safe job and our family had to do whatever we could to survive.

I learned many great lessons from my father, not the least of which was that **you can fail at what you don't want, so you might as well take a chance on doing what you love.**

I watched the effect my father's love and humor had on the world around me, and I thought, 'That's something to do, that's something worth my time.'

...When I was about 28, after a decade as a professional comedian, I realized one night in L.A. that the purpose of my life had always been to free people from concern, like my dad.

What's yours? How will you serve the world? What do they need that your talent can provide? That's all you have to figure out. As someone who has done what you are about to go do, I can tell you from experience, the effect you have on others is the most valuable currency there is.

Everything you gain in life will rot and fall apart, and all that will be left of you is what was in your heart. My choosing to free people from concern got me to the top of a mountain. Look where I am — look what I get to do!

…My soul is not contained within the limits of my body. My body is contained within the limitlessness of my soul —

…Our eyes are not only viewers, but also projectors that are running a second story over the picture we see in front of us all the time. Fear is writing that script and the working title is, 'I'll never be enough.'

This is the voice of your ego. If you listen to it, there will always be someone who seems to be doing better than you. No matter what you gain, ego will not let you rest. It will tell you that you cannot stop until you've left an indelible mark on the earth, until you've achieved immortality. How tricky is the ego that it would tempt us with the promise of something we already possess…?

…So I just want you to relax—that's my job—relax and dream up a good life!
…You are ready and able to do beautiful things in this world and after you walk through those doors today, you will only ever have two choices: love or fear. Choose love, and don't ever let fear turn you against your playful heart."

As you go through your day today, it's important to ask yourself the question, "Am I doing this out of fear or love? Am I making this decision out of fear or love?"

And lastly, we're going to reflect on some Biblical verses. There is one thing that Jesus said almost more than anything else. And that is "Do not be afraid". Because fear prevents you from becoming the person you were created to be. It prevents you from being fully alive. Here are a few selections of verses to think about from the Bible:

"For God has not given us a spirit of fear, but of power and love and of a sound mind." 2 Tim 1:7

"There is no fear in love. But perfect love drives out fear, because fear has to do with punishment. The one who fears is not made perfect in love."- 1 John 4:18

"Even though I walk through the valley of the shadow of death, I will fear no evil, for you are with me; your rod and your staff, they comfort me."-Psalm 23:4

""Have I not commanded you? Be strong and courageous. Do not be terrified; do not be discouraged, for the Lord your God will be with you wherever you go."-Joshua 1:9

So what are you going to be afraid of today? Making offers? Risk? You're not going to be afraid of anything because there is nothing to be afraid of. It's just a house. We're going to be making offers in a way today that are really low risk. But just remember this: Knowledge of something always always ALWAYS decreases the risk. We can decrease the level of risk all the way down to zero. But ultimately, it's going to come down to you conquering your fears and taking action.

5:30am-6:00am- Exercise and Stretch

Now that you are mentally prepared, push yourself a little extra in your workout today, whatever it is that you do. Is there an exercise you're afraid to do for whatever reason? Do it. For example, I'm afraid to do squats. I'm afraid because normally when I do squats my legs are sore for days and it makes it hard to even walk. I frickin HATE it! And it scares me! Ha!

So I get in a habit of skipping leg day. But here's the thing. If you are trying to build muscle, all the experts will tell you that squats are one of the most important things that you can do. It actually, somehow helps all the other muscles in your body grow as well and makes all your other workouts more effective. So I skip leg day because I'm afraid of being sore and it ultimately affects the effectiveness of all of my other workouts throughout the week.

Here's the reality about squats. The more I do them, the less sore I will get over time because the muscles will get more used to being worked out. So if I just pushed through my fear I would have tremendous results in all other aspects of my workouts. Whatever it is you have been avoiding in your workouts, do it today. That will help hammer home the theme of today's mindset and give you the mental stamina to accomplish your other goals in real estate.

6:00am-7:00am- Learn How to Take a Calculated Risk

In the show, each contestant had to be very smart about what they were going to risk doing. They could climb a mountain to get a better view of where to set up camp, but if they hadn't eaten in a while, they risked going into a calorie deficit by exerting too much energy. If they needed to find food offshore, and they made a canoe out of wood and tarp, they had to calculate the risk of going across rough seas and make sure that they launched when the tide was right, or they would fall into the freezing waters and risk hypothermia. Each action, carried a certain risk that needed to be calculated.

There is a really awesome trick you can use in real estate to completely eliminate your risk when making offers. Traditionally, you write a purchase agreement when you offer to buy someone's property. That purchase agreement may have an earnest money deposit for which you would have to write a check. And that agreement is legally binding. This is the risky way to go out and make offers.

The secret to making tons of offers in real estate without risking anything is to use what is called a "Letter of Intent" or LOI for short. And if you don't have one yet, you can go to the resource page to see where you can get a downloadable sample you can use.

You can send a Letter of Intent as an email or an attachment to an email, or you can fill it in on the spot when you visit a motivated seller. At this point, you have already talked to the motivated seller, and you are ready to make an offer, so you simply can send them an email with your offer to start the negotiations.

After they look at your offer, they can accept, reject, or counter offer. They might do this by calling you or emailing you back and you can hammer out the details right away. After you sign the letter of intent and they sign the letter of intent you can move forward with a purchase agreement. The cool thing about a letter of intent, is that it is exactly that. You are INTENDING to purchase the property under a certain price and under these certain terms. However, you are not legally bound to those terms. It's when you sign the purchase agreement that you are legally bound. So this is how you make offers with zero risk.

7:00am-9am- Start Constructing Your Offers

In the show, everyone had a different strategy for making a tent. They would use certain architectural angles and techniques to ensure that their shelter could weather the storms, keep in heat, and keep out rain and smoke. It was a really cool art form to watch.

In real estate, you will learn right now the art to negotiating and structuring offers. The first technique we are going to use is the "2 Offers Technique". Remember, there are two things that we can do with every single property that has a motivated seller. #1) We could make them a cash offer at 75% of the appraised value minus any repair or renovation costs. In this scenario, we could either have a private money lender finance it for us, or we could wholesale it to a Cash Buyer. #2) We could get them to Owner Finance the house to us using a lease option. In this way, we can turn around and sell it to a potential Owner Financed Buyer with no money out of our own pocket. So when we present an offer to a Motivated Seller, we are going to make 2 offers at the same time. 1) An all cash offer, and 2) An owner financed offer.

Math makes money. So let's look at a hypothetical scenario here and walk through the math so you understand how to make your offers.

Hypothetical Scenario: Lady Going Through Foreclosure- You were able to get in touch with a lady who is about to get foreclosed on. She is behind $2600 on back payments to her mortgage company. She lost her job 6 months ago and her husband divorced her and took the kids. Her life is a mess right now and the house is just one more stress she doesn't need. The house is worth $200,000. The balance on her mortgage is $134,000, and that includes paying back the $2600 she owes in back payments. Her mortgage, plus taxes and insurance every month is $1300 a month. The rental rates in the area are around $1600 to $1800 a month. The house wasn't in bad shape, but definitely needs in your estimate about $8,000 worth of minor renovations. Her motivation is that she just wants to be done with it and hopefully not damage her credit by declaring bankruptcy. It would also be nice if she had some money to get a small apartment to get back on her feet. What is your offer?

Let's look at our cash offer first. That's simple. We're going to take 75% of $200,000 which is $150,000. Then we are going to subtract from that $8000 worth of work giving us an all cash offer price of $142,000. This would give her $8000 as well in her pocket to help her start recreating her life. $142,000 would allow us to wholesale this to a cash buyer for $152,000 and make a spread of $10,000.

Next, we need to figure out our creative financed offer. We need to be able to make at least $10,000 from this deal. So at minimum our offer would be to have a lease purchase price of $190,000 less the renovation costs and less the back payments owed to the mortgage company. So really, the lease purchase price would be at least $179,400 to factor in $8000 worth of renovations and $2600 of back payments. Because if you turn this around to a lease option buyer, you will still need to put $8000 into it in order to attract a decent buyer who has cash to put down. She also needs to cover at least $1300 a month in rental payments.

Also, a typical owner financed offer is held as an owner financed offer for 3 to 5 years before the "buyer" is expected to refinance the home through a traditional lender and pay off the balance. This is called a "Balloon Payment". Once you get the house, you're going to finance it to someone else for 3 years. But you want to make sure you have some cushion in there for yourself. So between you and the Motivated Seller, you want to negotiate at least a 5-year balloon payment.

Also, on a typical lease option contract you have something called "rent credits". This is similar to an amortized loan where a certain amount per month goes toward principle and a certain amount goes towards interest. The lease option keeps it simple. It says, every month you are going to get $X towards the purchase price of the house. So when you go to cash the original owner out 3 to 5 years from now, you are going to pay the owner the sales price minus the down payment (aka. option payment).

There is no rule as to what the monthly rent credits can be. It can be 100% of the rent you pay goes towards paying down the sales price. Or it could be $0 a month. This is where you can get really creative with the math and make it work for you.

So here is how I might structure the owner financed option with this lady:

Sales Price: $179,400 (Ultimately this will give her more than the cash offer, but over time. And it will allow me to turn around and get an owner financed buyer.)

Option Payment Due at the Act of Sale- $2600 (To catch her up on her back payments). It's important to note, that since you are starting with no money, unless there is a back payment that is necessary to catch up on, you will just not even include this as part of the offer. I only included it here because it's necessary.

Monthly Rent-$1350 (I could just offer her the $1300 she owes per month, and I would, if there was no wiggle room in the rent that I could make. But because I know I can rent it for $1600 to $1800 a month, I'm going to increase my offer just a little bit to increase my chances of getting the deal with her. I might even be willing to negotiate this up to

$1500 a month just to get the deal done because I can still cash flow. But my initial offer will be $1350.

Balloon Term- 5 years. I am going to owner finance it to someone else for 3 years, so I want to make sure I have a little cushion in between.

Monthly Rent Credits- $500 a month. My strategy here is that I want to make sure I have 25% equity in the house at the end of 5 years, so I will have no problem refinancing the balance owed with the bank. I'm just going to reverse engineer my rent credit with present day values. It will be worth $200,000 all fixed up. I will need to only owe $150,000 at the end of 5 years. My offer was $179,400, so I will need to bridge the gap between $179,400 and $150,000. The number that will bridge that gap is $29,400 ($179,400-$150,000) that I will need in rent credits. $29,400 over the course of 5 years is $490 a month ($29,400 divided by 5 years divided by 12 months). I'm just going to round up to $500 to make it a nice even number to my benefit.

A quick note here. It is not an uncommon practice for real estate investors to ask for the ENTIRE monthly payments as a credit towards the purchase. Use your judgement here. It just depends on the motivation of the seller. It might work for them.

My hypothetical offer here would look like this:

Option A: $142,000 cash.

Option B: Owner to Finance with The Following Terms:

- Purchase Price: $179,400
- Option Payment- $2600
- Monthly Rent- $1350 a month
- Balloon- 5 years
- Monthly Rent Credits- $500 a month

Right now, you should have a pretty good idea and strategy in structuring your offers. Take a look at all the potential deals you have on the table and structure an offer to send out today for each of them.

9am-12pm- Make Offers

This is where the money is made right here. There is a specific art to this. The important thing to remember here is for you to be able to articulate **what's in it for them (WIIFT).** Nobody cares about what's in it for you. They only care about what's in it for them. So as you make offers, you need to get good at explaining what's in it for them.

Here is what an email would like for this hypothetical situation:

"Hi Jane, thanks for showing me your property yesterday. After reviewing the market comps, I would like to give you two different options that may work for you, and that would work for me based on my investment criteria.

The first offer is a straight cash offer. The second offer is an owner financed offer that might also be very beneficial for your situations.

Option A: I would like to offer you **$142,000** in cash. This would enable you to get out of the house as soon as possible. I can close in about 10-15 days, and in that time you would be able to pay off your back payments, and have $8000 to move on to the next chapter of your life.

Option B: I want to offer you an owner financed deal. This is where you basically become the bank to me on your house. The real benefit of doing this is that it will improve your credit. Because not only will I pay off your back payments, but I will also be able to give you more on the purchase price and you will be making a little passive income every month as well.

Here's what it would look like:

Purchase Price- $179,400
Option Payment- $2600 to be applied towards your back payments.
Monthly Rent- $1350 This will give you an extra $600 in passive income per year.

Monthly Credits Towards Purchase- $500 to be applied to the purchase price.

Balloon- 5 years. At the end of 5 years the entire purchase price will be paid off by me refinancing through a traditional lender.

At the end of 5 years, I estimate you will have made **$28,400**. That's $3000 in passive income from the monthly rent payments and estimating that you will have paid the loan down by about $10,000, you will make about $25,400 when I refinanced through a traditional lender after 5 years.

I will be responsible for absolutely everything. If the AC breaks, I will fix it. If the roof needs repair, I will repair it. If an insurance claim needs to be made, I will pay the deductible. All you have to do is watch a check go into your bank account once a month. The rent will be paid through a 3rd party escrow company, so they will take my payment, and pay your mortgage company in your name first, and then pay you what is left over after. Because the payment is still being paid every month in your name, you will have the benefit of your credit score improving.

If I fail to pay (which I won't), you can take the property back and keep the option payment. Worst case scenario, your back payments are caught back up and you own the house again.

If this looks good to you, I can draft up a formal offer within 24 hours and get started. I do have other properties that I will be making offers on today as well. So the sooner you can get back to me the better.

Feel free to give me a call if you have any questions. I hope I get to work with you on this and that it will help out your situation.

Sincerely,
Ryan"

That's it! Say a prayer and send that bad boy out. Construct all of your offers on all the potential deals and email them out right now and just see what happens. You can expect more people to say "no" than "yes". But that's why it's a numbers game. The more offers you make, the more you increase your chances of getting a yes or starting negotiations.

What if they say "no"?

Then no worries. Move on to the next one. I do think it's important to not burn a bridge on the deal though. You may have a Motivated Seller that is only a little motivated right now. Motivation increases more as time goes by without getting a deal on their house. And the more time goes by and they increase their days on market, the harder it becomes to sell a house. Time is on your side when making offers. You just have to be patient.

What I like to say if someone rejects my offer is something like this:

"Thanks for your time, Jane. I completely understand. I'm just not able to deviate from my investment criteria here. If you find that down the road you aren't getting any other favorable options to you and you wish to reconsider my offer, I'd be happy to entertain it with you again at that time. Please do keep my contact info just in case. I wish you the best! Take Care!

Ryan"

You would be surprised at how many people come back a couple weeks to a month later with increased motivation ready to accept your original offer.

12pm to 1pm- Continue to check all your nets and lines and make sure they are up to date, and that you are continuing to follow up with people and grow your list and make appointments.

1pm to…………..Wait…..Hold up! What's that in your inbox? 2! Not 1, but 2 people accepted your offer!

It's just one of those things in life that when it rains it pours. In the show, they would put out their fishing lines. But if they just sat there and waited and waited for a fish it would feel like forever. To keep sane and not focus on their hunger, they would do other things to stay productive. Go grab some firewood. Set another trap. Whittle a spoon out of a tree branch. They would do whatever they could to mentally stimulation themsleves.

And then all of a sudden....BAM! They catch a fish. And typically, it's not just one. The tide came in, and the fish are biting. So they catch another. And another. And another!

While you are waiting to see if you have an accepted offer, you're increasing your skills with practice. You are filling your mind with knowledge. You are continuing to scan for deals, cash buyers, and potential owner financed buyers. You're networking and growing your lists.

And then all of a sudden, you get an accepted offer! And then another. And then another! It always seems to happen that way. Get ready. Because when it rains, it pours.

So, you got 2 verbally accepted offers in your inbox. One of them was an owner financed offer, and the other was all cash. Now what?

Let's start with the all-cash offer. The next thing you want to do is draw up a purchase agreement. There are 2 main things you want to include in this purchase agreement to increase your chances of making money on it, and to avoid risk.

Make sure you give yourself at LEAST a 10-day inspection period. If you can get 15 or 20, even better. During these 10 days you are going to go find a Cash Buyer. This is also your way out if you need one. If after 10 days you can't find a Cash Buyer, you can cancel the agreement, and site any reason due to the inspection.

You want to add contingency clauses, also known as "weasel clauses". It's named that because it gives you the opportunity to "weasel" out of the contract. Don't let the name turn you off to it. It's just a protectionary clause for you to get out of contract if you need to. There are things in purchase agreements that protect sellers, and this is just a protection for you. In the additional terms and conditions section of the purchase agreement you can add clauses that you can use to get out of the contract before the inspection date ends. Here are a few that I use:

- Subject to the review and approval of my partner.
- Subject to review and approval of neighborhood comps

- Subject to review and approval of renovation costs from a licensed contractor

Next, after you have written the purchase agreement, you will want to meet the motivated seller at a public notary to have the purchase agreement notarized. This is an extra precautionary step, but because you will be showing the deal to other cash buyers, you don't want any of the parties to eliminate you illegally as the middle man. Just as an extra precaution, get the contract notarized, and then go down to your county recorder's office and have the county clerk record the document. That way, nobody will be able to get the property under contract without you because your document will show up in a title search and they won't be able to close without you.

A little extra advice here: Always be honest with the Motivated Sellers on what you will do with the property. That way, it's not a big surprise to them if you wholesale it or if you get in another lease option tenant on top of your lease option. I always like to say right before signing the purchase agreement something like this:

"I'm glad we can work this out. I just want to be clear here that I am a real estate investor and my intention with the property is to make money. That could be wholesaling it, getting another lease option on it, or renting it out, or something else. Just want to make sure you're ok with me exercising all options available to me as an investor on this property."

Alright, now let's take a look at the owner financed offer. There are a couple of steps you will want to take here outside of getting the contract signed.

You will want to call your new buddy at the title company and ask him if he can recommend an escrow service for the monthly payments. You don't want to be paying them and then they turn around and pocket the cash and never pay their mortgage. The escrow company is absolutely necessary because they ensure everyone gets paid: the home owner, the mortgage company, the insurance company, etc. You pay them first. Then they will turn around and pay the mortgage, insurance, and taxes on the property. Then whatever is left over, the escrow company will pay to the seller. If the title company doesn't recommend one you can just search "escrow services" on Google and find a company. Expect to pay $15 to $50 a month for the service. You could possibly negotiate that the seller has to pay this as well.

You will want to send your title company the terms of the lease option that you negotiated and the contract and ask them if they will help you close the deal. Send them the lease option agreement available to you from the resource page and ask them if it needs to be customized to fit local law.

You do not need a title company to close a lease option. You can close it in a day without doing a title search.

When I am selling property on lease option, I don't even involve the title company. But when I'm buying on lease option, I always get the title company to do a search. Because you never know what kind of liens or judgments they might have on the property that would ruin the deal. There may be some minimal title charges, but you will want to factor the cost of this when you look for a down payment from someone else.

After the title company gives you back an airtight lease option agreement, you want to go get it signed and notarized. The execution date of the agreement, can be 10 to 20 days from the signing. This will give you time to go out and find an Owner Financed Buyer. Just like the cash offer purchased agreement, you are going to want to go down to the county recorder's office and record the document to protect yourself.

That just about wraps up the day! Get the contracts signed at a public notary if you can. And if you can't, still get them signed and try to arrange to meet at the notary later. Congratulations! You have 2 deals in hand. Time to work on the battle plan to find buyers for these deals.

5:15pm-6pm- Reflect on the Day

Your hard work is paying off. Taking action is paying off. Trusting the blueprint is paying off. You are a few days away from securing not only $10,000 on a wholesale deal, but ANOTHER $10,000 on a lease option to a tenant buyer (Owner Financed Buyer)! Lots to be thankful for today. You've learned how to structure and make offers. You've practiced the math. And more than anything, you didn't let fear get in the way of moving forward so you could have these awesome opportunities in hand. It feels like flying out of an airplane right now.

Following our usually routine, spend time reflecting:

- Did I do everything in my control to hit my goals today? If not—what do I need to focus on improving tomorrow?
- Did I learn something new?
- Did I do something outside my comfort zone?
- What was my area of genius today?

DAY 5
Burn the Boat!

5:00am-5:30am- Coffee/Prayer/Reflection

Today's success all comes down to one thing: *resourcefulness*. You have TWO CONTRACTS IN HAND with the potential for WAY OVER $10,000, which was your goal. You need to stop at nothing in order to find a Cash Buyer and an Owner Financed Buyer, also known as a Tenant Buyer.

Today's reflection to chew on comes from Tony Robbins telling a story to a foreign audience about a conference he did in California:

"Who here's ever failed? And no one raised their hand in the whole room. So I pause and I said, I know you're out there, I can hear your hearts beating. Who here has ever failed? And I demanded an answer and then a few people raised their hand. I said, who here's ever failed? And now they all started complying. So I said great, when you failed, why did you fail?

And they said all the things you said. Didn't have enough time. Didn't have the right technology. Didn't have the money. Didn't have the contacts. You know, had the wrong people. The people said we had the wrong leader, right?

And then this voice in the darkness, the whole room was pitch black, says I didn't have enough Supreme Court Justices. And I looked down and it's Vice President, Al Gore. Who you probably don't know much about American politics, but he and Bush Jr., they tied basically. It had to go to a Supreme Court to decide who's gonna be it and he lost. And when he said that we were in northern California, which is all Democrats, would've been supporters of his, they all stood up and gave him a standing ovation when he said this.

So when they stopped the standing ovation I said, that's one way to try to explain why you didn't become President of the United States. But I wouldn't say it's an accurate one. And there was this pause, like what is he about to say? And I said, 'cause let's just do this logically. Everything you people have told me, I didn't have the technology, I didn't have the right contacts, I didn't have the time, I didn't have money. Everything you've told me, I didn't have enough Supreme Court Justices, those are resources. And so you're telling me, I failed 'cause I didn't have the resources. And I'm here to tell you what you already know. Resources are never the problem, it's a lack of resourcefulness is why you failed.

Because the ultimate resources are emotional states. Creativity, decisiveness, passion, honesty, sincerity, love, these are the ultimate human resources. And when you engage these resources you can get any other resource on earth. Resourcefulness is the ultimate resource. And if you don't have what you want, stop telling yourself a story because you don't have the money, you don't have the time, that's bullshit. It's because you haven't committed yourself where you would burn your boats. If you want to take the island, burn your boats and you will take the island. 'Cause people when they're gonna either die or succeed, tend to succeed."

The interesting thing about the show, Alone, is what makes some people quit when others keep pressing ahead. If you want to succeed, burn your boats. I wonder how long these contestants would have gone if they didn't have a button they could push at any time to save them. It's interesting what excuses they gave for quitting.

In season two, within the first couple weeks of him being on the island, the winner fell into the water. He was at risk of hypothermia. All of his clothes were wet. But in his mind, he had "burned the boats". So he just committed to drying himself off in his tent next to a fire and try to fight off hypothermia.

By contrast, the guy who ALMOST won in the final days, also fell into the water. At that moment, he pressed the button and quit. He gave the excuse that he had no choice, but we had all seen the winner face the same choice. He could have used the same resources as the other guy to dry himself off and press on. But he just hadn't mentally burned his boats to say that no matter what, he was going to use the resources around him to succeed.

You are ALMOST there….You are at the final stretch. You have not one, but TWO contracts in hand. And now, you just have to be as resourceful as possible to find a buyer, and you WIN. So commit yourself today to pressing on no matter what with your resourcefulness.

5:30am-6am- Exercise and Stretch

If you really want to hammer home this theme in your brain of resourcefulness, do some sort of workout like Rocky did in Rocky 4. You remember that one? Probably one of the best Rocky movies ever. This is where he fights the Russian, Ivan Drago. This movie was timed perfect with history because it was released close to the time of the Cold War between the Soviet Union and the United States.

Anyways, Rocky is of course the underdog. And during the workout training scenes, you see Ivan Drago using all of the latest technology. By comparison, Rocky doesn't have access to all of that high-tech equipment because he is fighting Drago on his home turf. All he has been given is a log cabin in a snow filled wasteland of nothingness.

During the training scene, you see Drago on an electric stepladder, and a multitude of doctors are analyzing the data of his heart rate and strength on some expensive tracking equipment. Then you see Rocky running through the snow uphill alone. You see Drago running around an indoor track as trainers surround him with stopwatches. Then you see Rocky running around a frozen stream outside. You see Drago doing a series of leg and arm workouts with wires attached to him. Then you see Rocky lifting a horse and carriage that had fallen over in the snow, sawing logs, and chopping wood. And of course (spoiler alert) Rocky, with his resourceful training beats the Russian, even though he had all the latest and greatest resources available to him.

Haha! I'm not saying you have to do any of this. Sometimes it helps to put mindset into action in the little ways. So if you can't find someone in a horse and buggy that just fell over in the snow today that might help you with your leg presses, maybe just go running outside today instead of on a treadmill.

6am-8am- Prepare how you are going to market to your Cash Buyers and Owner Financed Buyers.

Let's start with finding **a Cash Buyer** for the $200,000 house that you got under contract for $142,000 and needs $8000 in renovations. The first thing you will need to do is create a one sheeter that lays out the opportunity to your cash buyers.

It should have what you are willing to sell or assign the contract for, the ARV of the home, the estimated renovations, and comparable properties and rents in the area. It doesn't have to be complicated at all. In fact, it has to be the opposite of complicated. It has to be simple, and clearly outline the opportunity for the cash buyer.

Here is an example of one that I did a while ago:

5012 Anthony Lane #16
Covington, Louisiana
Price: $130,000

Living Square Feet: 1348
Bedrooms: 3
Bathrooms: 2.5
Year Built: 2005

Estimated Repairs and Renovations:
Touch up paint and cleaning $1000
New carpet on stairway and in bedrooms $1000

Total Estimated Project Investment: $132,000

Range of Price Per Square Foot Sold in Past Year Very
Good to Excellent Condition:
$108 to $112

After Renovation Value Range:

$145,500 (VRGD Condition)
$160,000 (Excellent Fully Renovated Condition)

Estimated Profit: $23,000

Return On Investment: 17.42%

	4005 JONATHON LN 55	4053 JONATHON LN	2012 CHRISTIE LN 4
Address	4005 JONATHON LN 55	4053 JONATHON LN	2012 CHRISTIE LN 4
Ref #	936240	937552	961413
Status	Sold	Sold	Sold
Area	204	204	204
Subdivision	Fairway Garden Homes	FAIRWAY GARDENS	FAIRWAY GARDENS
City	Covington	COVINGTON	Covington
Bedrooms	3	3	3
Full Baths	2	2	2
Half Baths	1	1	1
Condition	EXCE	EXCE	EXCE
Living SqFt	1,388	1,377	1,375
Lot Size	35 x 65 Apprx	35 X 65	35 X 65
# Acres	0.000	0.000	0.000
Lot Desc	Condo	Condo	Gated Community
Type	PAT	TNH	SGL
Age	7 /Renovated cosmetic changes of	7 /Renovated cosmetic changes of	8 /Renovated cosmetic changes of
Car Storage	One	Garage	Driveway Only
Fireplace	Gas	Gas	Yes
Exterior	Vinyl Siding	Brick	Stucco, Siding
Foundation	Slab	Slab	Slab
Roof	Shingle	Shingle	Shingle
Appliance Incl		Dishwasher, Microwave	
Pool Type	CO	CO	CO
A/C	Two, Central	Central, Two	Central, Two
Heating	Central	Central, Two	Central
Gas Type	Natural	Natural	Natural
List Price	$149,900	$159,700	$159,900
LP/SqFt	$108.00	$115.98	$116.29
List Date	12/17/12	01/07/13	08/07/13
Condition	EXCE	EXCE	EXCE
Sold Price	$149,900	$155,000	$152,300
SP/SqFt	$108.00	$112.56	$110.76
SP/LP Ratio	100.00%	97.06%	95.25%
Contract Date	03/01/13	02/05/13	09/13/13
Sold Date	03/22/13	03/01/13	10/03/13
DOM	74	29	37

So just open up a word document and create something like this. I had a realtor email me the comps. You can do that or copy and paste some comps from Zillow. If you want, you can also add the repair estimate from homewyse.com as well.

After you have prepared the one sheeter that you will send out to all of your cash buyers, go ahead and create a listing on Craigslist for your **Owner Financed Buyers**. You want to list is under homes for rent AND homes for sale.

After you are done listing it there, you can copy and paste the same content and put it on Facebook marketplace and Zillow under for a sale or for rent. Here is an example of one of my listing:

Schedule an appointment or submit an application today! This deal won't last long and you don't want to miss out!

There are many reasons people aren't able to get conventional bank financing right now. Don't let that stop you from owning this home. Here are your options:

Option A: 20% Down
Purchase Price: $239,000
Down Payment: $47,800
Monthly Payment- $1700 (includes taxes, insurance, etc)
Monthly Credit Towards the Purchase: $250 ($3000 per year)
Balloon- 3 to 5 years until you have to refinance to a traditional lender.

Option B: 10% Down
Purchase Price: $239,000
Down Payment: $23,900
Monthly Payment- $1800 (includes taxes, insurance, etc)
Monthly Credit Towards Purchase: $200 ($2400 per year)

Option C: 5% Down
Purchase Price: $239,000
Down Payment: $11,950
Monthly Payment- $2000
Monthly Credit Towards Purchase: $150 ($1800 per year)

Option D- Straight Lease: $2100 no option to purchase

There is a certain art to advertising a house that is available for lease purchase. If you notice in my description of the house above, I give the potential buyer 3 different options. They can either put 20% down, 10% down, or 5% down, and then I give them an option for a straight lease.

In our scenario with Jane, we have to come up with at least $2600 for an owner financed cash buyer, or else we won't be able to pay her the back payments. There are no rules in how to structure this. In the future, you will probably want advanced training on how to structure this, but here are the basics.

Just a reminder, these are the terms you agreed upon with Jane:

Purchase Price- $179,400

Option Payment- $2600 to be applied towards your back payments.

Monthly Rent- $1350 This will give you an extra $600 in passive income per year

Monthly Credits Towards Purchase- $500 to be applied to the purchase price.

Balloon- 5 years At the end of 5 years the entire purchase price will be paid off by me refinancing through a traditional lender.

If you remember, the house needs $8000 worth of minor renovations and is worth $200,000. You are going to present this to the potential owner buyer as "price includes an $8000 budget to customize your own colors for paint, and install $4000 worth of granite"…something like that.

Your purchase price is always going to be $200,000 or more. Being that you will owe $179,400, that means you will have $20,600 in equity in the property ($8000 of which will need to go to repairs).

This means you will need to ask for an option payment between $18,000 and $20,600 in order to achieve your goal to make at least $10,000 on the deal. $20,000 would only be 10% of the purchase price. That's a good deal for a tenant buyer who can't get a conventional loan from the bank that would want 20% down.

If you remember, based on your market research, you could get $1600 to $1800 in rent. So you would want your option payment to reflect your rent. In other words, if they only gave you $18,000, then you would charge them the higher rent at $1800 a month. If they gave you $20,600, then you would maybe charge them a little less in rent down to $1600. Either way, you are going to be making $250 to $450 a month in passive income.

You would not want the monthly credits of the tenant buyer to exceed YOUR monthly credits. You are getting $500 a month. I would give them between $150 and $250 per month. You also want to follow the same formula on the rent payments. For a higher option payment, your credits will be higher. For a lower option payment, your credits will be lower.

For the balloon, you want to give them 2 to 3 years before they have to refinance through a traditional lender. Remember, you have it for 5 years. If they default, you want to give yourself somewhat of a cushion to find another tenant buyer again.

By the way, you might think it's a bad thing if someone defaults. It's actually great for you financially. Because once they default and leave the house, you get to keep their $20,000 option payment and do it all over again with someone else. That's how you turn a property into a cash cow. I have actually had one property default 3 times. The first time I kept $20,000. The second time I kept $30,000.

And the fourth time, I kept $40,000 as an option payment that the tenant/buyer defaulted on.

So go ahead right now and create a listing on Craigslist and structure an owner financed offer for the property. Giving them an option A, B, and C works best.

8am-5pm- Market to the Cash Buyers and Owner Financed Buyers

The first thing you are going to do is start with the lists you created. Let's look at your Cash Buyer list first. One thing that is important to understand is that you need at least 10 cash buyers on your list in order to be as successful as possible. Why? Because the only reason a cash buyer wouldn't wait 10 days for your contract to expire is because they are afraid of losing the deal to another cash buyer. Why would they pay you an extra $10,000 if there were no other buyers? If there are no other buyers, and they were sharks (which they sometimes are) they would just wait for the contract to expire, eliminate you as the middleman, and get the contract directly from the owner.

So you want to shoot out an email to a large number of Cash Buyers. And that group email or group text should look something like this:

"Subject Line: $200,000 house for $152,000!

Hey Everyone,

If you are getting this message it is because you are on my buyers list of cash investors that are interested in discount properties. Well, I currently have an amazing deal under contract. A $200,000 house that I can do a double sale or assignment contract for $152,000.

Attached you will find a one sheeter of the details of the property, the estimated renovations, and the comps to support the price.

I'm sending this out to a list of all my cash buyers, so it will be first come first serve if you are interested. If after reviewing the numbers you want to setup an appointment for tomorrow, the process is to send me proof of funds, and I can be reached at 555-555-5555 to setup the appointment

Sincerely,
Ryan"

You always ask for proof that they actually have cash to close because you don't want people wasting your time and kicking tires if they don't actually have the money to do it. Hit send, and if you did the right steps to create a great list, you can watch the feeding frenzy start. But you don't want to limit yourself to just this list. You have to be aggressive and resourceful. So you want to use every free source available to you to get the word out about your deal.

- Make a Craigslist post- $200,000 home for $152,000!
- Make as Facebook post on your personal profile- $200,000 home for $152,000! If any of you guys know anyone who wants a great deal send me a PM.
- Go into Facebook groups like local real estate groups and post the same thing- $200,000 house for $152,000. Cash buyers only! Contact me asap if you are interested.
- Start calling cash buyers on your list in case the email went to spam
- Start calling people within your network. Tell your title attorney, your bankruptcy attorney, the people you met at the real estate investment club that you just got an amazing deal under contract if they know of any cash buyers who may be interested.
- Go onto real estate forums like Bigger Pockets and see if you can touch base with some people there.
- Go onto LinkedIn and let everyone know

I'm sure I haven't covered every possible channel here. But you get the point. Use all the resources at your disposal until you find a cash buyer.

OK, now let's talk about how to market to your Owner Financed Buyer (Tenant Buyers). The first thing you're going to do again, is tap into your existing list that you have been creating and send out an email to them. The email should look something like this:

"Subject Line: Opportunity to Become a Home Owner Through Owner Financing

Hi Everyone, if you are getting this email it is because you have shown interest in becoming a home owner again through an owner financing program.

Maybe you have credit repair needed. Maybe you don't have the W2 income that the banks like to see, but you do have a down payment, and are waiting for the opportunity to start building equity in a home and growing your wealth.

I've got the perfect opportunity for you! This home is in (x) neighborhood. For details on this home and how you can get into it TODAY, contact 555-555-5555 and check out the Craigslist link below for pictures and details. (link to Craigslist ad you created)

If you are interested, act fast, because there are many on this list, and this is a tremendous opportunity to become a home owner again without banks while growing your wealth and/or improving your credit at the same time.

After reviewing the listing, if you are interested, the next step would be to set up an appointment to see it with me and execute a lease option application with me.

Sincerely,

Ryan"

Go ahead and send that out now. And then you want to utilize the same resourcefulness you used above to find a Cash Buyer.

- You want to make Facebook posts on your personal profile. "Just got an amazing house in a great neighborhood. If any of you guys know of anyone who is currently renting but would like to become a home owner, I am willing to owner finance this house to them."

- Post that same message out to your networks, your online threads

- Start calling people on your list in case them email went to spam

- Put a flyer out at the local grocery store.

- Stick a sign in the ground "Lease to Own house. Call 555-555-5555". This method is actually incredibly effective, but it is illegal in most counties and you could get fined. Plenty of people do it anyways, and if you're desperate to find a buyer, you might be willing to take this risk.

Do whatever you need to do to get a tenant buyer FAST. When someone replies back to you that they are interested, you will want to send them a lease application, so you can get an idea of their price range and see how much money they have to put down on it.

Just do a Google search for your states standard rental application. Then at the top of the rental application, write, "Which option are you interested in?"

Here is an example of a previous email I have sent out to Owner Financed Buyers for a $300,000 home:

"Please submit the below application to me via email. I will need copies of your last two paycheck stubs and your taxes from last year. I will also need you to go onto Experian.com and send me your credit report. If your credit is in need of repair, that's ok. I have designed this program to assist with that. The credit report will tell me how far we need to go to repair your credit before you are able to refinance to a traditional lender.

Thanks

Ryan

Please select which option you are applying for:

Option   A:
Purchase   Price: $299,500

Downpayment(10%)- $30,000
Monthly   Payments- $2000
Monthly Credit Towards Purchase Price- $250 ($3000 per year)
Term of Lease- 3 years or sooner if able to refinance sooner.

Option   B:
Purchase   Price: $299,500
Downpayment   (7.5%)- $22,500
Monthly   Payments- $2100
Monthly Credit Towards Purchase Price- $200 ($2400 per year)

Option   C:
Purchase   Price: $299,500
Downpayment(5%)- $15,000
Monthly   Payment- $2200
Monthly   Credit   Towards   Purchase   Price- $200
Term of Lease- 3 years or sooner if able to refinance sooner

LOUISIANA RENTAL APPLICATION
Equal Housing Opportunity. Please Complete All Information Below.
Applicants Full Name_____
Phone #_____DOB_____
Social Security #_____
Drivers License #_____State_____Exp._____

CurrentAddress _____
City_____State_____
Zip_____
Current Landlords Name_____

Phone #_____How long at this address_____ Reason
for leaving _____
Previous Address_____City _____State_____Zip_____
Previous Landlords Name_____Phone #_____How long
at this address_____Reason for leaving._____
Auto Yr_____ Make_____Model_____
State/License Plate #_____
Employer_____Position_____
Annual Income_____ Employers
_____Address_____
City_____State_____
Phone #_____
How long at job_____Other _____

Do you smoke? ( ) Yes ( ) No

Have you ever been evicted?[]Yes []No

Have you ever been convicted? [ ] Yes [ ]No

If Yes to any of these, you may explain here:

Preferred move-in date ____

Number and type of Pets_____

 Name of bank_____

Branch____Type of Account____ Name of bank___Commerce
Bank_____Branch_____Type of
 Account_____ Personal

References
Name _____Yrs.
Known____Relationship_____Phone #_____
Name_____Yrs. Known____Relationship__Phone
#_____
Name_____Yrs. Known__Relationship_Friend__Phone
#_
Total number of adults___, total number of children living
with you under the age of 18_____
Names and relations of all other applicants

_____, _____,

_____

Annual Income of Other Applicants_____

I CERTIFY that answers given herein are true and complete to the best of my knowledge. I authorize investigation of all statements contained in this application for tenant screening as may be necessary in arriving at a tenant decision, I understand that the landlord may terminate any rental agreement entered into for any misrepresentations made above.

Applicant
Signature_____Date_____ "

So just find your local state rental application, add the options on the top to see what kind of down payment they can afford, and set the expectation of what you need to see from them as far as credit and income is concerned.

As a rule of thumb, you want their income to be at least 4 times whatever you are going to charge in rent. Otherwise, it's going to be tough for them to pay and may give you an issue down the road. The credit score is less concerning. Because you are going to ask for a large down payment, there is less of a chance of them defaulting on you. But if they DO default, you keep that down payment in the form of a defaulted option contract.

5pm-6:00pm- Reflect on your day

Today was another amazing day. You have several interested parties and a few appointments set for tomorrow for both houses. The check is so close to your hand that you can almost taste it. You learned today what to do to motivate

Cash Buyers and Owner Financed Buyers to be interested in your property. You learned how to structure your marketing efforts. And above all else, YOU BURNED YOUR BOATS and didn't quit! You used all the resources available to you. You planted the seeds, and tomorrow, you're going to bring in the harvest big time!

Time to reflect once again:
- Did I do everything in my control to hit my goals today? If not—what do I need to focus on improving tomorrow?
- Did I learn something new?
- Did I do something outside my comfort zone?
- What was my area of genius today?

DAY 6
Reaching Your Limitlessness

5:00am-5:30am- Morning Prayer/Reflection

Today is payday! Today is the day to smash the negative things that you believe about yourself once and for all. I've seen it too often at this phase. Where someone has a great deal, but they also have a habit of having negative thoughts and end up sabotaging themselves with their limiting beliefs.

Once you realize that your thoughts start to become your reality, you can be aware of all the ways that you think that limit yourself. If you didn't have these thoughts, or beliefs about yourself, you would accomplish so much more and become the best version of yourself. Instead, sometimes we become the limited version of ourselves because of the thoughts we have in our head.

Today is the first day of many that we will become the best version of ourselves by creating repetition and habits of success. Instead of worrying that you might not get the deal today. You are going to imagine what it's like to actually GET the deal, and hold the check in your hand, so you can program your subconscious mind like a heat seeking missile to navigate around any obstacles until you hit your target.

Perhaps one of the most popular "limiting beliefs" was the idea of the 4-minute barrier. For the longest time, runners believed that running a mile in under 4 minutes was humanly impossible. This is what motivational speaker, Les Brown had to say about it:

"Before April 1954, the common belief, the universal belief because it had been tried again & again & again, and people had failed the belief was that man was not physically capable of breaking the 4-minute barrier, that he could not run a mile in less than 4 minutes. When something happens to them, they begin to believe that that's the way it is. That's the way it's always been. And they can't see the possibility of it being any different.

Roger Bannister came along, and he broke the 4-minute barrier! Since that time, up to this day, over 20,000 people have done it... including high-school kids! Twenty thousand people! What changed? Here's what happened when they got on the track: They knew it had been done! And because they knew it had been done, there was a new belief! ...about this barrier that was 'unreachable'.

And those twenty thousand people got in a race believing and knowing in their heart that someone had done it that it's possible that they could do it. And I'm saying that if you know anybody that had some goal, some dream something they wanted to do, and they did it, then I'm saying that you know in your heart, if someone has done it, then YOU can do it. It's possible. And that, if someone can make THEIR dream a reality, then it's possible. You can make YOUR dream become a reality.

And so, as you begin to look at where you want to go, and you begin to embrace that, it's possible. 'I'm blessed and highly favored. I've got a lot going for me. I've got some good stuff in me. It's possible that I can bring my greatness out here in the universe. That I can do what I want to do. It's possible. I can write my own book. I can open my own business. I can take the trip and travel around the world. It's possible. I can bounce back from adversity and reinvent my life. It's possible. Regardless of where I am, things can get better for me.' It's possible!"

Today can really go either way. It's how you set your mind this morning that will determine the outcome. So, program your brain right now with the idea that you are going to get your houses under contract and receive a check. The 4-minute mile barrier has already been broken. People execute wholesale deals for over $10,000 every day. People execute sandwich lease options every day for more than

$10,000. Not only is it possible, but with the way you are going to set your mind today....it's probable.

5:30am-6:00am- Exercise and Stretch

Is there anything you have been eliminating from your workout because you didn't think you could do it? Do it today.

6am-8am- Prepare your expectations and strategize how to close the deals.

Let's start with the Cash Buyers. This one is pretty easy. You're going to let the potential Cash Buyers see the house, and then when it's done, they can decide whether or not they want to move forward with your price. Remember, your real leverage here is only if you have multiple Cash Buyers interested. That way, you can get your price, and you don't have to worry about them waiting until your contract ends with the seller. Whoever is eager for the deal will pull the trigger today on it.

What you want to do is contact the Motivated Seller and ask them if you can get a key to the property to view it with contractors, other potential investors and inspectors. You ask it this way, because it would be preferable if the motivated seller isn't there when you show the property. It's not a real big deal if they are present at the property, but it's just better when they aren't. So, when you ask to get a key, that indicates that they won't be there.

You want to set up a time with the Motivated Seller that you can show the property to a potential fellow investor, inspector, or contractor, and try to get in the house to show it today. One technique that ads urgency to getting the offer is to tell all the cash buyers to meet you at once. Telling them that there are other people looking at the property is one thing. Letting them see that there are other people looking at the property is another.

It prevents the typical negotiative talk from them about how crappy the property is and that it's not worth the price, or the renovations are going to cost more than projected, blah blah blah. If you did your homework right, it IS a good deal, and not only will you get a Cash Buyer to put it under contract right then and there, but you may create a feeding frenzy and have cash buyers bid up the price!

Now let's talk about the second house you have under contract that needs an Owner Financed Buyer (Tenant Buyer). You have several people potentially interested. Again, see if you can contact the motivated seller and arrange a time to show it without them there. And see if you can line everyone up to look at the house at the same time.

For both of these appointments today you will want to come prepared with a blank purchase agreement and a blank lease option agreement. Take some time now to print a few copies out, and practice writing each one out and explaining the contract as if you were doing it live. Practicing it at least once will give you confidence to look like a pro when you do it.

8am-10am- Show the first property to Cash Buyers

You have 5 Cash Buyers interested, and they are all going to be coming by between 8am and 10am to see the property. All of them show up at the same time and you let them look around. Some of them ask you about the motivation of the seller and why they are selling it. Some are performing their own personal inspection on it.

At the end of it, you have 2 investors interested! One guy wants to flip it. The other guy wants to hold it and rent it out because he knows he can get great rents in the neighborhood. The guy who wants to flip it offers you your asking price. The guy that wants to hold it and rent it out knows it's an amazing deal and he can afford to pay it down over time with the renter's monthly rent payments, so he offers you $5,000 OVER the other guy!

Heyo! Congratulations! You just locked up a contract for $15,000 profit! Whether you use an assignment contract or just another purchase agreement for a double closing will depend on the conversation you had with your title attorney. You just move forward with whatever process your title attorney advised you to do, and you send him all the contracts, so he can begin working on it. The closing date is set for 7 days from now.

11am-1pm- Show the 2nd Property to Owner Financed Buyers

You have 8 people interested in buying the property in which you executed the lease option. You've already pre-qualified them, and all of them have between $18,000 and $20,600 in an option. You end up getting two people that are pretty motivated to lock the house up and move in as soon as they can.

One has bad credit, but a large down payment as an option payment. The other doesn't have as large of an option payment but can afford a higher rent per month then the other guy. You end up making a decision on who to rent to right then and there.

You are getting $20,000 down as an option payment, and $1800 a month in rent. This will give you an additional $450 a month in cash flow! You both hop in the car and plan to meet 30 minutes later at the public notary to give him time to go down to his bank and get a certified check for $20,000.

1pm-5pm- Execute the Lease Option Agreement and Take Payment

You go down to the notary to sign the lease option, cash his check, and let him know he'll be able to get into the house in 15 days, which is when he can pay the first month's rent. You set him up with direct deposit through your bank so that his payments are automatically drafted every month from his account to yours. You start having a conversation with them about the renovations and they let you know what they want to spend their $8000 budget on.

In the meantime, you let the motivated seller of the property know that you are ready to execute the closing with them as soon as possible. With the money you just got as a down payment, you execute the Lease Option. Boom!

5pm-6pm- Reflect on the Day

All you can say is, "Ho-ly CRAP THAT WAS AN AWESOME DAY!" You just made $15,000 on a wholesale deal set to close next week. You cashed a $20,000 certified check TODAY. Subtracting the 8k renovations and $2600 back payments, that's $9400 profit. PLUS, you set yourself up to make an extra $450 a month in passive income cash flow (an extra $5400 a year). So today you generated a total of $24,850 for this month. If you can do that in just 6 days, imagine what you could do in 365 days!

Time to reflect once again:

- Did I do everything in my control to hit my goals today? If not—what do I need to focus on improving tomorrow?
- Did I learn something new?
- Did I do something outside my comfort zone?
- What was my area of genius today?

DAY 7
Going from Surviving to Truly Living

5am-10pm- All you have to do...is REST!

That's all you have to do today. Taking the biblical principle of resting on the 7th day, you are going to rest today. I heard somewhere that the rest isn't for God. It's for you! You hammered away at this week and now it's time for your mind, body, and spirit to just relax, recuperate, and rejuvenate.

Be grateful for an amazing week. Be at peace knowing that you can provide. Not just in the short term. But in the long term as well with passive income streams. And look forward to doing the same thing next week!

St. Irenaeus said, "The glory of God is man fully alive." Now is the beginning of how you are going to make the switch from just surviving, to actually LIVING.

Figure out today how you will serve the world with your freedom. Albert Schweitzer said, "This much I know. Those of you who will truly be happy will be the ones who have sought and found a way to serve."

What's Next? Your 365 Day Plan

One thing that the survivalist understands is that they can start their life out of nothing if they need to. It isn't about what you have. Whatever you don't have, you can get. It's about being resourceful.

One of the biggest lies out there is that it takes money to make money. It obviously doesn't, and I just showed you how it doesn't. However, it is also absolutely true that when you have money, it is a lot EASIER to make money. It would have been way easier for the contestants on "Alone" to survive if they weren't limited to a little survival backpack, but instead, had a pontoon boat, a gas station, an Academy Sports, a grocery store, and an ATM machine with $10,000 in their account.

Barry Sanders, the famous running back for the Detroit Lions, used to say that if you want to learn how to run fast, practice sprinting uphill. This battle plan is designed for you to go through the exercise of real estate investing starting with nothing. Sprinting uphill. But after you're done, how much faster are you going to accomplish your financial goal if you are on a level playing field? Say you have money. Well, your mission to achieve financial freedom just got a heck of a lot easier. You just got a lot faster sprinting from point A to point B.

The next step, after this battle plan is to see what strategy you can use to completely replace your working income with passive income in the next 12 months or less. Because the point of all of this, isn't to just survive, but to have enough passive income to live the life of your dreams. On the resource page, you will see other educational opportunities that will get you from A to B as fast as possible.

And lastly, the show wasn't called "Alone" for no reason. They could have called it many other things. "Survival Challenge"! Or "Last Man Standing"! or some other survival theme. They called it "Alone" because that is what the survival came down to. When they were past the 30-day mark, it was no longer about knowing the strategy to survive. It was no longer about the skills that they needed. And for the most part, it wasn't entirely about the mindset.

After 30-days, it was about doing it all alone. That is what made even the best survivalists quit. Fortunately, you DON'T have to do this alone. There is no shortage of groups, clubs, mentorship programs, etc. that you can be a part of that will help you on your journey to financial freedom. In my experience, the people who are able to achieve financial freedom in 12 months or less through real estate had all of the elements below:

- Contracts
- Investor tools
- The right strategy
- The right mindset
- The desire to finesse and practice the skills
- The desire to invest in themselves to acquire knowledge
- The support of an experienced investor and mentor
- Accountability to achieve their goals
- A great network with which they could surround themselves

For more information on everything at your disposal, check out the resource page that follows.

RESOURCES

**CASHFLOW FREEDOM
ACADEMY**

CashFlow Freedom Academy - If you are a normal person with an average to above average human brain, you probably had a question or two, or *one hundred and two* questions as you read this book. That's why real estate mentorship exists because there are so many questions throughout the process. CashFlow DadLife has set up an amazing program that will provide you the answers and guidance of a personal mentorship without the cost. To learn more about the 12 month strategy we use in the academy (which is different than the 30 day strategy of this book), and how we can help you become financially free in 12 months or less, you can visit cashflowdadlife.com/freedom. In this training, I will show you EXACTLY what I did to make $387,000 in passive income in less than 12 months.

Secret Weapon Training- In order to execute this blueprint, you will need the lease option contract and the training on how to utilize it. You will also need a sample Letter of Intent, a Standard Purchase Agreement, and a Contract Assignment. If you want these contracts and the in depth training on how to use them, you can go to cashflowdadlife.com/secretweapon

Free Real Estate CRM- Podio

Renovation Cost Resource- Homewyse.com

Marketing- Craigslist.com, Zillow.com, Redfin.com, Facebook.com

Networking- Biggerpockets.com

Free Craigslist Scraper- iftt.com

Map Quest Route-Planner-
https://www.mapquest.com/routeplanner

Find a List of Cash Buyers- Listsource.com

Paid Services:

If you have a small budget, and you want to advance to using some tools that will make this process easier for you. Here is what I recommend:

PropStream- This is an amazing software program that we use to find lists of motivated sellers, figure out how much they owe on the property, and have access to MLS data. For a free 5-day trial, check out: https://cashflowdadlife.com/propstream

REFERENCES

Alone (TV Series). Leftfield Pictures. 2015

Kiyosaki, Robert. Rich Dad Poor Dad. Warner Books Ed. 2000.

"How To Do The Thing You're Afraid To Do - Feat. Elliott Hulse". YouTube. 2017.
https://www.youtube.com/watch?v=7aIOTxy2pII&feature=youtu.be

"CHOOSE FRIENDS WISELY - MOTIVATIONAL SPEECH FOR SUCCESS". YouTube. 2017.
https://www.youtube.com/watch?v=JTx8x6t91eU&feature=youtu.be

"What Skydiving Taught Me About Fear | STORYTIME". YouTube. 2017
https://www.youtube.com/watch?v=bFIB05LGtMs&feature=youtu.be

"Jim Carrey - Choose Love not fear". YouTube. 2014.
https://www.youtube.com/watch?v=EEXaNY5lKTQ&feature=youtu.be

"Rocky vs Ivan Drago (Rocky IV) - Training Montage HD 720p". YouTube. 2014. https://www.youtube.com/watch?v=gqwuYX3fZZc&feature=youtu.be

"What is the ultimate resource for success? | Tony Robbins". YouTube. 2016. https://www.youtube.com/watch?v=OHNfqdL9_1Y&feature=youtu.be

"MOTIVATION If Someone Else Has Done it, You Can Do It! MUST SEE Best motivation Les Brown". YouTube. 2013 https://www.youtube.com/watch?v=LweYBcVI5N8